Mysteries and Secrets R

The

Gundam

Explorer

Wing, First, G, SEED and more!

cocoro books

Published by DH Publishing, Inc.
2-3-3F Kanda Jimbocho, Chiyoda-ku
Tokyo 101-0051, Japan
www.dhp-online.com

cocoro books is an imprint of DH Publishing, Inc.

First published 2004

Text and illustrations ©2004 DH Publishing, Inc.

Printed in USA

Printed by Delta Printing Solutions, Inc.
Compiled by Kazuhisa Fujie and Martin Foster
Publisher: Hiroshi Yokoi
Publications Director: Clive Victor France
Design: Kyoichi Akimoto
Editor: Takako Aoyama

ISBN 0-9723124-8-X

The Gundam Explorer:
A Must For All Gundamaniacs!

In this book, the first in the "**Mysteries and Secrets Revealed!**" series, you'll find everything you need to know about Gundam First, Wing, G, SEED and much more! And it's so easy to use! Just follow the simple Gundam Explorer code below and within a few hours you'll be a Mobile Suit master.

Questions and Answers
Want to find out why who did what when and where? Then this is the book for you. 52 questions and detailed answers on every topic, from characters and relationships to weaponry and wars.

Glossary
When you speak the lingo everything is so much easier. At the back of this book you'll find a glossary stuffed full of names, what they mean and which pages to find them on.

Keyword Index
Want to go straight to A Baoa Qu? Then start at the alphabetical Keyword Index at the back of the book. There you'll find page links to every destination in the Gundam universe.

Gundam Files
Scattered throughout the book are 15 Gundam Files that introduce you to the wackier side of Mobile Suit Mania. Check out Pepsi's Gundam bottle caps, Gundam at school, Gundam goods, Gundam stamps, Char jeans, Gundam models, Gundam cosplay, Gundam fortune-telling and Gundam pachinko!

Contents

Mobile Suit Gundam SEED

and more

Gundam Files

The Four Parallel Worlds of Gundam

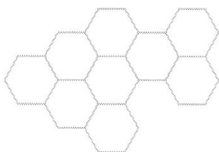

Broadly speaking, the Gundam series can be described as eclipsing four parallel worlds. There is Mobile Suit Gundam from the Universal Century (UC), Mobile Fighter G Gundam of the Future Century (FC), Mobile Suit Gundam Wing of the After Colony (AC) period and Mobile Suit Gundam SEED from the most recent series, which hails from the Cosmic Era (CE). All are tales of the near-future, a time in which almost all humans inhabit deep space.

It is, however, in the early series, set in the Universal Century, where the world view is laid out in most detail. Human beings construct colonies in space to cope with the overflowing population of Earth, the plan being to have a share of the Earth's population live there. Thus, the first year that humans migrate to space and begin living there becomes Universal Century Year 1.

The first part of the Gundam series,

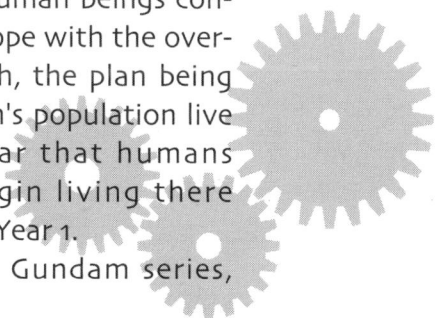

Mobile Suit Gundam, is set in the UC Year 79. However, the period leading up to UC Year 79 is also recounted in great detail. It is an important prologue to the entire series and gives the Gundam series the realism it is so admired for.

So, let's first return to the period between the start of UC and the arrival of Gundam.

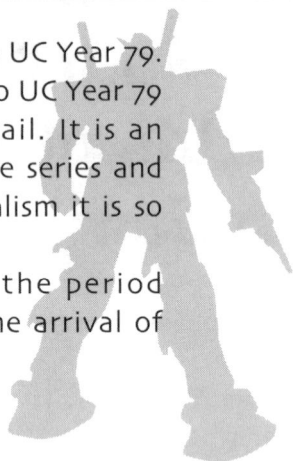

Mobile Suit Gundam

The Earth Federation is responsible for the planning and implementation of the Space Colonization Program, which has been established to save Earth from pollution and over-population. In the period immediately following the declaration of UC Year 1, the space emigrants are being closely controlled by the government.

However, by the year UC 40, things have changed radically. A number of colonies have already been established and over half of mankind is now living in space.

The cause of this sudden leap in numbers is the corruption of the Earth Federation's colonization policy. The de facto policy has switched from the ideal of preserving Planet Earth to a practice of driving the masses into space. The colonies have become virtual slave nations, leaving only a privileged class on Earth.

This is the seed of the independence movements that begin to form among the settlers of the colonies, who grow dissatisfied with the policies of the Earth Federation.

In the UC '50s, a revolutionary named Zeon Daikun emerges in Side 3, a colony that had seen a marked move toward independence. In UC 58, he establishes the independent Republic of Zeon. This sends a tremor through the other colonies, which leads many to also consider independence.

To preempt any further schism, the Earth Federation sets out to crush the independence movements with military force.

However, while this is taking place, discord is rising in the Republic of Zeon between Zeon Daikun and his right-hand man Degwin Sodo Zabi. By the UC '60s, Degwin Sodo Zabi - whose ultimate plan is to become dictator of the independent state - has gained control over the armed forces, and the Republic and the Earth Federation have become engaged in a furious arms race, expanding armaments and developing new weapons. In UC 73, the independent colony, now known as the Principality (or Duchy) of Zeon, achieves its goal of developing the first mobile suit (MS).

Two years later, Degwin Sodo Zabi has mass-produced the combat-ready Zaku mobile suits and begins a war of independence against the Earth Federation. This is the outbreak of a conflict that becomes known as the One Year War, and so begins the story of Mobile Suit Gundam.

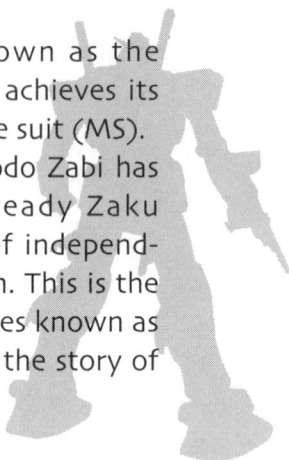

Mobile Fighter G Gundam

While the Future Century of Mobile Fighter G Gundam is described as a far-off time in much the same way as UC was, it aims at a much more simplified history. The general feeling was that UC had become too complicated.

FC Year 1 sees the outbreak of the Earth Chaos War, as settlers, although having migrated to the space colonies, are unable to shake off their earth-bound attachments to notions of nation and state.

The Earth Chaos War turns out to be a more tragic, terrible war than anyone could have imagined, and it is this that leads to the introduction of the Gundam Fight as an alternative to war itself.

The inaugural Gundam Fight is fought in FC 8 as a proxy war between Gundams representing each nation to decide who will control space. They are repeated every four years, in much the same way as the Olympic Games are. Mobile Fighter G Gundam is the story of the 13th tournament in the year FC 60.

Mobile Suit Gundam Wing

The story of Mobile Suit Gundam Wing is based largely on the After Colony (AC) period. The story of the struggle between the space settlers and the privileged classes who remain on Earth also falls broadly into this period.

The colonies see the rise of the peace-loving ruler Heero Yuy, whose ascendency brings security and a greater respect for law and order. However, when Heero Yuy is assassinated, the Romefeller Foundation embarks on a war with the colonies. The foundation has been a major financial backer of the United Earth Sphere Alliance and looks to assume control of the alliance's military forces for its own personal gain. Mobile Suit Gundam Wing is the story of the characters caught up in this era.

Mobile Suit Gundam SEED

Mobile Suit Gundam SEED, from the most recent series, hails from a time known as the Cosmic Era (CE). The main difference between this series and the others that came before it, with the exception of G Gundam, is that it introduces normal human beings, or "Naturals," and genetically enhanced "Coordinators" into the equation of the battle between Earth and the colonies.

The idea of the struggle between Earth and the colonies equalling that between Naturals and Coordinators is a progressive world view, one that is in line with the new-era Gundam.

Gundam Series Chronology

Universal Century (UC)

0001: Commencement of space migration. Total Global population tops nine billion.

0010: The Jupiter Energy Fleet is reorganized as the Jupiter Development Enterprise Group.

0016: The Earth Federation establishes the Frontier Settlement Transport Bureau.

0027: Von Braun City, the first permanent lunar settlement, is completed.

0030: The Earth Federation privatizes the Frontier Settlement Transport Bureau. Establishes the Space Transport Enterprise Group.

0034: The Earth Federation reorganizes the Space Transport Enterprise Group. Establishes the Public Corporation of Space Transport as an NGO.

0035: Construction of Side 3 begins.

0040: Some 40 percent of the global population completes its migration to space.

0045: The asteroid Juno (later to become Luna 2) is placed into Earth's orbit. The Minovsky Physics Society is established on Side 3.

0047: Development of Minovsky-Ionesco type thermo-nuclear reactor begins.

0050: Total world population reaches 11 billion people, of which nine billion have migrated to space.

0051: The Earth Federation announces a freeze on development of new colonies.

0052:	Zeon Zum Daikun relocates to Side 3.
0055:	The Buffo Conzern is established.
0058:	Zeon Zum Daikun declares independence for Side 3. Republic of Zeon is established.
0059:	The Earth Federation applies economic pressure on Side 3.
0060:	Earth Federation forces set into motion the armaments build-up program of the '60s, particularly in relation to the space fleet, converting Luna 2 into a military base.
0062:	Zeon National Guard elevated to National Army.
0068:	Death of Zeon Zum Daikun. Degwin Sodo Zabi assumes position of prime minister.
0069:	Declaration of Principality (or Duchy) of Zeon.
0070:	Ducal military successfully tests the Minovsky Effect.
0071:	Zeon ducal forces commence development of new weapons based on the Minovsky Particle.
0072:	Zeon ducal forces begin construction of the asteroid base Axis in the asteroid belt.
0073:	The Principality of Zeon completes the first prototype mobile suit, the MS-01.
0079:	The Principality of Zeon declares independence from the Earth Federation and subsequently declares war, launching a simultaneous surprise attack that is the outbreak of the One Year War.
0080:	One Year War ends.

Future Century (FC)

| 0001: | High ranking government officials and the upper classes from various countries move to colonies based on original concepts |

	of nation and state.
0002:	The outbreak and intensifying of Earth Chaos War. Increased risk of thermo-nuclear warfare.
0004:	End of Earth Chaos War. The colonies bring the various countries of the Earth under their direct control. The colonies aggressively compete to develop next-generation mobile suits. Commencement of operational experiments of MS on Earth.
0006:	Colonies commence development of leading-edge MS to be known as Gundam. A United Colonies Federation military adviser named Professor E.C. Ducer proposes the Gundam Fight.
0008:	1st Gundam Fight (Won by Neo Greek Vulcan Gundam)
0012:	2nd Gundam Fight (Won by Neo American Gundam Freedom)
0016:	3rd Gundam Fight (Won by Neo Egyptian Pharaoh Gundam III)
0020:	4th Gundam Fight (Won by Neo Chinese Feilong Gundam)
0024:	5th Gundam Fight (Won by Neo French Baron Gundam)
0028:	6th Gundam Fight (Won by Neo Italian Gundam Tornado)
0032:	7th Gundam Fight (Won by Neo German Kaiser Gundam)
0036:	8th Gundam Fight (Won by Neo Russian Cossack Gundam)
0040:	9th Gundam Fight (Won by Neo England Britain Gundam)
0044:	10th Gundam Fight (Won by Neo England Britain Gundam)
0048:	11th Gundam Fight (Won by Neo England Britain Gundam)
0052:	No Gundam Fight
0056:	12th Gundam Fight (Won by Neo Hong Kong Kowloon Gundam)
0059:	Ultimate Gundam developed on Neo Japanese colony. The

Ultimate Gundam is seized by Kyoji Kasshu, son of the inventor, and taken to Earth, where it becomes the Dark Gundam, and sets out to destroy humanity.

0060:   13th Gundam Fight (won by Neo Japanese God Gundam)

After Colony (AC)

001:     Humanity begins its move to space from Earth

102:     Some 15% of humanity lives in space as colonists. Endless disputes on Planet Earth signal the start of a 50-year period of uncontrolled carnage.

130 - :   Earth-bound disputes die out.

133:     The United Earth Sphere Alliance established. Quells disputes with overwhelming military power.

139:     Colonies establish a system for colonial self-government.

145:     The emissary of Planet Earth is attacked in space en route to the L1 colony cluster, and goes missing.

147:     With its overwhelming military power, the United Earth Sphere Alliance forcibly establishes a military presence in the colonies in the name of justice and peace.

149:     Beginning of second great wave of space migration. Emergence of catch-phrase "Space harbors unlimited possibilities and gold."

165:     Emergence of Heero Yuy as leader feeds into renewed sense of solidarity between the colonies.

175:     Heero Yuy assassinated. As a result, the colonies fall into a state of chaos in the absence of a central binding force.

176:	The United Earth Sphere Alliance dispatches troops to the colonies again. All colonies placed under oppressive military control.
180:	The Romefeller Foundation sets out on a project to adapt mobile suits, which have been used for work in space, for use in battle.
182:	The United Earth Sphere Alliance intervenes in the affairs of the northern European nation Sanc, setting off a coup d`etat.
193:	Treize Khushrenada becomes leader of the secret military society OZ.
195:	Operation Meteor begins. The five Gundams are dispatched to Earth.
196:	Colony L3-X18999, led by head of state Mariemeia Khushrenada, declares independence from the United Earth Sphere Alliance and embarks on war.

Cosmic Era (CE)

70:	Economic friction leads to antagonism between the Naturals of the United Earth Sphere Alliance and the Coordinators of ZAFT (Zodiac Alliance of Freedom Treaty). Leads to the Bloody Valentine Incident.
71:	War breaks out between the United Earth Sphere Alliance and ZAFT. ZAFT raids the Alliance, and steals four of their five secret prototype Gundams.

Model: MGRX-79 (G) Ez 8
Scale: 1/100
Built by RUN

Mobile Suit Gundam

Broadcast on Japanese TV from April 7, 1979 to January 26, 1980.

Overview

The trail-blazing opening series of the Gundam saga. No one on the production team could have guessed that the show would become so popular, spawning series after series. In fact, this first Gundam series was not an immediate hit with anime fans. The secret of its eventual success was clearly in its revolutionary view of a new world, one that includes the concept of mobile suits and the clash between the space colonies and the earth.

Story

It is year 79 of the Universal Century (UC) and Side 3, a space colony, assumes the title of Principality (or Duchy) of Zeon, and sets out on a war of independence from the Earth Federation. After a round of early fierce fighting, the war declines into a quagmire, which lasts for eight months. The Federation begins the development of top-secret mobile suits (MS) on Side 7, looking for a military breakthrough. However, the secret is leaked, and Side 7 comes under surprise attack from the Principality of Zeon. Side 7 becomes a battleground, and the civilian, Amuro Ray, pilots the Mobile Suit Gundam and destroys the Zeon Mobile Suit Zaku. Meanwhile, civilians are trapped on board the Federation's mobile assault carrier, White Base, as it drifts from battle to battle.

Main Characters

The Earth Federation

Amuro Ray, Bright Noa, Sayla Mass, Mirai Yashima, Matilda Ajan, Kai Shiden, Hayato Kobayashi, Ryu Hosei, Sleggar Law

The Principality (Duchy) of Zeon

Char Aznable, Lalah Sune, Degwin Sodo Zabi, Gihren Zabi, Kycilia Zabi, Garma Zabi, Ramba Ral, Crowley Hamon, Dozle Zabi

Civilians

Fraw Bow, Katz Hawin, Letz Cofan, Kikka Kitamoto

Main Mecha

The Earth Federation

RX-78 Gundam, RX-77 Guncannon, RX-75 Guntank, RGM-79 GM

The Principality (Duchy) of Zeon

MS-05 Zaku I, MS-06F Zaku II, MS-06S Char's Zaku II, MS-07B Gouf, MS-09 Dom, MS-14 Gelgoog, MS-14S Char's Gelgoog, YMS-15 Gyan, MSM-03 Gogg, MSM-04 Acguy, MSM-07 Z'Gok, MSM-07S Char's Z'Gok, MSM-10 Zock, MSN-02 Zeong

Main Vehicles

The Earth Federation

RB-79 Ball, FF-X7 Core Fighter, G-Armor, Assault Carrier White Base, Cruiser Salamis, Battleship Magellan

The Principality (Duchy) of Zeon

MAM-07 Grabro, MAX-03 Adzam, MA-04X Zakrello, MA-05 Bigro, MAN-03 Braw Bro, MAN-08 Elmeth, MA-08 Big Zam, Light Cruiser Musai, Mobile Cruiser Zanzibar

What events lead to the One Year War? 1

The One Year War is a savage conflict that pits Side 3, the colony which had earlier declared itself the independent Principality (or Duchy) of Zeon, against the Earth Federation.

Of the two principal factors that lead to the war, we can point to the high-handed attitude of the Earth Federation toward the colonies as the most obvious.

The Space Migration Program is undertaken by the government of the Earth Federation in an attempt to tackle the overpopulation that threatens the planet. Eventually, however, the egos of a number of earth-bound bureaucrats get the better of them, and they begin treating the colonizers as if they are slaves. This leads to widespread anti-government sentiment among the settlers, and the hostility eventually spills over into war.

However, for the direct cause of the war, the blame must rest with the Zabi family, which embarks on a series of armed incursions, verg-

See Glossary

House of Zabi
One Year War
Side 3
Principality (or Duchy)
of Zeon

ing on wars of aggression, to expand the area under its control. At its head is the independent state's supreme leader, Degwin Sodo Zabi.

The Principality of Zeon is originally established as the Republic of Zeon by the charismatic Zeon Daikun, the architect of independence from Side 3. Even in the face of the Earth Federation's oppression, Daikun believes in a peaceful resolution to the Republic's problems. However, with his sudden death in the year 68, all this changes.

It is not clearly spelled out in the story, but Daikun's unexpected death is considered to be the dirty work of Degwin Sodo Zabi, who, at the time, was Daikun's aide and number two man in the Republic.

And so it is that Degwin becomes the colony's dictator, changing its name to the Principality (or Duchy) of Zeon and assuming for himself the title of Archduke. With total power now in his hands, Degwin sets out to strengthen the military might of his new state with the goal of resisting by force the rule of the Federation.

This path leads to the invention of a new breed of super-weapons: mobile suits.

For five years, Degwin Sodo Zabi prepares for battle. On January 3, year 79 the time has finally come. Immediately upon declaring war,

See Glossary
Republic of Zeon
Zeon Zum Daikun
Mobile Suit

he unleashes his armies upon neighboring colonies. Indiscriminate slaughter soon follows. Within 48 hours, three colonies have been totally annihilated and three billion lives lost.

For the Federation, the effectiveness of this onslaught serves to highlight the power of the mobile suits. The Federation government had initially considered unconditional surrender. Now it decides on a policy of outright resistance. As a result, the conflict continues for a whole year, and becomes known as the One Year War.

The Federation intensifies its armaments development program in a bid to match the might of the Principality of Zeon. The result is the mobile suit Gundam, whose fated pilot is to be civilian Amuro Ray, the central character of Mobile Suit Gundam.

See questions
2 8 9 50

震える力宇宙　めぐりあえよ生命

Mobile Suit Gundam III:
Encounters in Space (1982.
Shochiku)
Director: Yoshiyuki Tomino
Production: Nippon Sunrise
141 min

Flyer (7~10 inch) $4.00

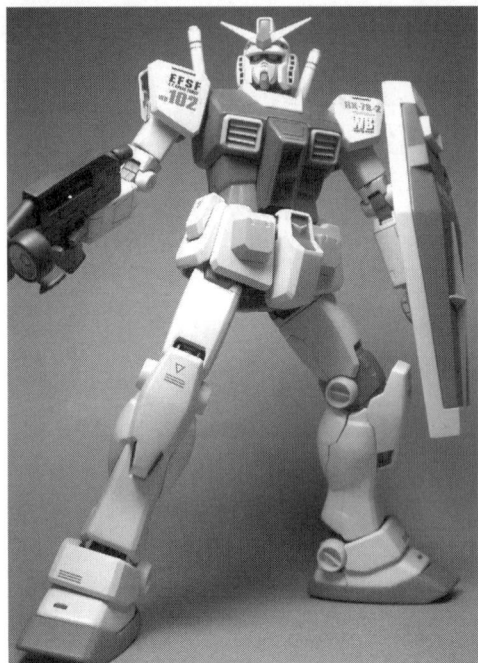

Model: MG RX-78-2 Gundam Ver 1.5
Scale: 1/100
Built by RUN

Why is Amuro Ray able to immediately pilot Gundam?

2

muro Ray's quite remarkable ability to pilot Gundam the moment he climbs in is often attributed to the fact that he's a "newtype" - an advanced human being with special abilities, such as superhuman reaction speeds and heightened powers of empathy and awareness. However, there is no proof that the two are related.

In fact, when he sets out to pilot Gundam, Amuro Ray is unaware of his newtype status and subsequesnt special powers. It is only after several mobile suit battles that he begins to realize his inner potential.

But, if it is not because of his newtype abilities, then how is it that untrained Amuro is able to almost instantly master MS Gundam simply by reading the manual - albeit a very long one?

Although Amuro is a gadget-loving kid and can fully understand what is written in the manual, it is the design of MS Gundam that makes it so easy to operate. So easy, in fact, that even an

See Glossary

Mobile Suit

inexperienced kid can jump into the cockpit and take it for a spin.

Gundam is mounted with a "self-learning" computer. Into this have been programmed many of its basic movements. The computer allows Gundam to judge one situation from another and, with simple commands from the pilot, determine the optimum course of action.

However, although Amuro's newtype abilities have little effect on his nascent piloting skills, in the latter half of the story, when he has awoken to his special powers, there is a considerable shift in his techniques. We see the speed of his responses accelerate to the point where, surpassing the Gundam computer, his powers of judgment are near-mystical.

See questions

1 7 9 38
50

Model: HGUC RX-77-2 Guncannon
Scale: 1/144
Built by Komochi-Shisyamo

Model: HGUC RX-75 Guntank
Scale: 1/144
Built by AKM

What is the Jupiter Energy Fleet?   4

I n the man-made space colonies, energy is created by nuclear reactors. However, the basic fuel of the reactors - Helium 3 - doesn't exist in the Earth Federation. The nearest large-scale deposits are on Jupiter, to which extraction expeditions are regulalrly sent.

In the world of the near-future depicted in Gundam, while it is relatively easy to travel around the Earth Federation - extending as far as the moon - it is still an era that necessitates the use of mamoth ships to get as far as Jupiter.

Indeed, the mining and collection of helium from Jupiter is a national project, one that has led to the creation of the Jupiter Energy Fleet. This convoy was designed as part of a national undertaking, and is recognized as indispensable to the continued existence of mankind.

However, because the fleet makes extended journeys into space, it has been rendered certain autonomous powers. As a result, administered by bureaucrats, the fleet has in time

See Glossary
Space Colony

See questions
8

become a powerful organization unto itself.

Model: HGUC GM RGM-79 GM
Scale: 1/144
Built by AKM

Why does Char wear a mask?   5

Char goes some way to answering this himself in episode 38, when he both poses and answers the question in explaining how he made the break with his past. "Why do you think I wear a mask?" he asks. "Because I have left my past behind me".

The implication is that the mask has allowed Char to become one with his new identity. But there is a less elaborate reason for him donning the mask - to conceal his true identity. For Char is, in fact, Casval Rem Daikun, son of Zeon Daikun and brother of Sayla Mass.

In so much as Char has disguised his identity with a mask and become a commander in the Principality of Zeon forces, we can also point to the revenge motive.

His father Zeon Daikun was assassinated by Degwin Sodo Zabi, and he understandably bears a grudge against the House of Zabi. Indeed, the major reason for his leaving Earth for space, entering Zeon and attending the officer training institute there was in order to get

See Glossary

Zeon Zum Daikun
Principality (or Duchy) of Zeon
House of Zabi

close to members of the Zabi family.

Char had an exceptionally brilliant career at the officer training institute and has received special dispensation to wear the mask. This is based on the belief that he has suffered an eye injury, lost some resistance to light as a result, and now requires an eye-protection glass.

In going this far to hide his identity, we can see that Char has effectively given over his life to exacting revenge from the House of Zabi. However, while garnering a distinguished war record as a Zeon pilot, he also begins to investigate the possibilities of an era when newtypes will dominate.

However, Char does eventually lose the will to revenge his father. While Char utters the words, "I have left my past behind me", at the outset of the story, his motive of, "To avenge the death of my father", is based almost entirely in that same past.

See questions
6 7 9 32 48

Model: HGUC MS-06S Char's Zaku II
Scale: 1/144
Built by Komochi-Shisyamo

6 How does Char's Zaku differ from others?

C har's Zaku II is characterized by its red color and feather-like communications antenna on its forehead. Nicknamed Red Comet for its speed and color, the Zaku is officially known by its product number MS-06S, a high-performance version of the mass-produced 06F model. It was not originally produced exclusively for Char.

See Glossary

Zaku
Red Comet

See questions

5 9 38

What kind of beings are newtypes? 7

To answer this question, it's important to look at the differences that separate such characters as Amuro Ray and Lahla Sun from ordinary human beings.

Firstly, there is the concept of "newtype". The term contains the nuance of an "evolved human being", which is based on the general idea of evolution of the species. The premise is that human beings who migrate into space and live there would, over time, undergo evolutionary change. From this would emerge a "new type" of human in much the same way new life forms emerged from the oceans.

Living in such a different environment as space would likely promote some kind of change in the human body. In Gundam, those human beings, who have adapted so that they can more easily live in space, become "newtypes".

When it comes to the question of what kind of adaptive changes humans would have to undergo, we find that in the world of Gundam it's all left a little fuzzy, with only vague references to beings with super-human powers.

This is the fault of the makers of the televison series Mobile Suit Gundam. When it was being aired real-time on TV, there was little viewer patience with the complicated structure of the Gundam world, which tended to act as a drag on viewing rates. This prompted the writers to conveniently explain away the concept of newtypes with such easily understood terminology as "super-human powers".

However, in later Gundam series, newtypes were positioned as "beings driven out to fight because of their special abilities, and as such deserving of our sympathy" - in effect, depicting their evolution as a curse.

Model: MG MS-07B Gouf
Scale: 1/100
Built by AKM

Still, the concept of mutation also exists in real-world biological evolution. Following the logic that those who evolve are those most adapted to their environment, it can be argued that newtypes are merely a single mutation in the evolutionary process, and have not necessarily undergone change that would alter the direction of human evolution entirely.

Therefore, when we consider the meaning of "newtype" within the confines of the Gundam series, it is preferable to simply think of it as a term applied to a person with powers that most people lack.

See questions
2 9 38

Model: HGUC MSN-02 Zeong
Scale: 1/144
Built by AKM

8 What kind of energy powers the mobile suits?

I n general, mobile suits are equipped with nuclear-powered engines. Within these are embedded extremely small nuclear reactors using Minovsky Particles that continually set off nuclear explosions. However, moblie suits do not appear to harness this explosive power as energy. Instead, the nuclear explosions produce massive electrical charges that drive the various motors throughout the suit.

Another energy system mentioned in the Gundam series is known as "Rocket Burner". It comprises rocket engines worn on the back and powered by liquefied fuel.

See Glossary

Mobile Suit
Minovsky Particles

See questions

3 50

Does Lahla fall in love with Amuro Ray at first sight? 9

With nobody to take care of her, Lahla is adopted as a young girl by Char, who first recognizes her newtype abilities. As she grows up she feels a sense of obligation to him, and is endlessly loyal. She also falls in love with him.

Lahla and Amuro Ray meet for the first time on Side 6. Lahla is waiting for Char to collect her, and meets Amuro by chance as he tries to shelter from the rain. The two are immediately aware of something special between them, and it's only after meeting Lahla that Amuro awakens to the full realization of himself as a newtype.

However, when Lahla and Amuro next meet, it is on the battlefield... and as enemies. For Lahla, who has sworn allegiance to Char, this is her maiden battle. Although inexperienced, she exhibits her newtype strengths by knocking out four warships in a single day.

But in her first face-off with Amuro, it is Char who loses out. He goes to her assistance,

See Glossary

Side

43

but is forced to retreat.

When they meet in battle the second time, Lahla loses her life to Amuro while attempting to defend Char. But again it is Char who suffers. During combat, Lahla and Amuro's exchanges are patently sympathetic, such as "You turned up too late!" and "This is our fate!" This drives Char into fits of jealousy.

Based on this telepathy between Lahla and Amuro, it was originally believed that Lahla had fallen in love with Amuro the first time they met, on Side 6. However, given later developments, when they both anticipate their "tragedy as newtypes", it is probably right to consider this merely the empathy between two new-

Model: MG MS-14A Gelgoog
Scale: 1/100
Built by AKM

types who are aware of their unhappy fates.

However, if we ask whether Lahla died defending the Char she loved, then we would have to consider Lahla's feelings towards Char - love, but also gratitude. It also seems Char's affections toward Lahla are influenced by what he views as an intriguing newtype specimen. This is especially so when we consider the jealous remarks he makes when Lahla and Amuro are communicating between themselves.

The character of Lahla is created to give expression to the unhappiness of the newtypes. Through Lahla, the writers have transcended the dimensions of love to appeal to the concept of fate.

See questions

2 5 6 7

Model: MG MS-09R Rick Dom
Scale: 1/100
Built by Komochi-Shisyamo

Gundam's Near-Death Experience

The story of Mobile Suit Gundam and mecha anime could have been oh so different. When the first series began on Japanese television in 1979 it met with such lukewarm a response that it was canned half-way through. However, not long after, the first MSG model kits hit the stores, rekindling an interest that had all but withered.

On the plastic heels of the model came three movies edited from the failed TV series - Mobile Suit Gundam, Mobile Suit Gundam: Movie II (Soldiers of Sorrow) and Mobile Suit Gundam III: Adventures in Space. Suffice to say, they were huge hits, igniting a boom in everything that had even a whiff of MSG. Today, with another TV series in the works even as this book goes to print, it is difficult to imagine how close we came to a world devoid of mobile suits.

Gundamaniac pop quiz: TV vs. Movie (answers at bottom of page)

1. To protect themselves when entering the atmosphere, what technology do MSGs use in a) the movie, b) the TV series?
2. What does Hayato Kobayashi pilot in a) the movie, b) the TV series?
3. In which medium do a) G-Armor and b) Core Booster appear?
4. In the movie, what is the name of Giren Zabi's secretary?

Mobile Suit Gundam (1981, Shochiku)
Flyer (7 x 10 inch) $4.00

1. a) cooling forcefield b) heat-resistant film
2. a) MSG b) Guntank and Guncannon
3. a) TV b) Movie
4. Cecilia Irene

46

Is it true that when the series was first aired it failed to make an impact? 10

Mobile Suit Gundam is now considered to be a masterpiece, with one series being made after another. But when it was first aired, viewers, mostly children, found it difficult to follow the realistic situations and complex storylines. The show didn't catch on, and as a result it was taken off the air after a premature final episode.

Still, there is an interesting coda to the series. Gundam was originally a low-budget production made with a small number of staff under extremely trying conditions. If anything, the screenwriter and director Yoshiyuki Tomino was glad when the project was halted.

Mobile Suit Gundam was unlike the conventional robot anime pattern of "robot as champion of justice takes on evil organization" that was standard viewing for kids. It also didn't follow the established sequence of introducing new robots with each episode. These factors are believed to have contributed to its initial low-key image and weighed on its popularity.

However, viewing rates picked up with each repeat series, and popularity increased. Indeed, when a number of the made-for-TV episodes were repackaged as the movies Mobile Suit Gundam, Mobile Suit Gundam: Movie II (Soldiers of Sorrow) and Mobile Suit Gundam III: Adventures in Space, they were immediate hits, making Gundam the archetype of the robot anime genre.

Also, unlike previous animated robots, Gundam was designed to have a strong 3-D effect. This was evident when the Gundam image was carried over into remarkably realistic models. In Japan, robots had mostly been designed by animators with an affinity for two-dimensional expression. This resulted in a sense of unnaturalness when their ideas were recreated as three dimensional toys. The "reality" that children discovered in their Gundam models fed into the increased popularity that followed.

Prior to Gundam was the experience of Space Battleship Yamato, which also failed to appeal to a wider audience on first showing, but saw a vast increase in popularity after the airing of repeats and the release of the movie of the same name. Yamato too suffered by having images overly based on realistic representations of the world. However, its detailed world view eventually caught the eye of the movie-going

See questions

51 52

public, and its popularity grew to the extent
that it returned again and again to TV.

Model: MG MSM-07 Z'Gok
Scale: 1/100
Built by Komochi-Shisyamo

Model: HGUC YMS-15 Gyan
Scale: 1/144
Built by Komochi-Shisyamo

Model: MG RGM-79 GM
Scale: 1/100
Built by RUN

Model: Operation V
Scale: 1/144
Built by RUN

Gundam File   002

Batteries Not Included

Weighing in at just over 66 pounds, standing 5 1/4 feet high, and with a width of some 3 feet, Hyper Hybrid Model is every Tokyo housewife's nightmare.

But it's not only size that makes this 1:12 scale a monster not to be messed with.

Priced at just under $2000, HY2M's 207 bolt-together pieces are made with the same cutting edge "blow form" technology used to mold race car aerodynamics. It comes replete with submachine gun and heat hawk, and is delivered in two 3ft-long boxes. And what's more, it's movable from the waist up!

Can it be many more years before full-size Gundam models stalk the toy store aisles?

Sight for Sore Eyes: This M06S Zaku II guards the entrance to a Tokyo optician's.

Mobile Fighter G Gundam

Broadcast from April 1, 1994 to March 31, 1995.

Overview

Produced to celebrate the 15th anniversary of the first Gundam series, Mobile Fighter G Gundam introduced a new story from an entirely different era to the previous series. It also introduced a plethora of new Gundam characters, and, combined with a bold production that saw the Gundams exhibit their fighting prowess to the max, became hugely successful.

Story

The curtain rises on the year Future Century 60. Six decades have passed since the Earth's elite began their migration into space, leaving the unfortunate masses behind to fend for themselves on the polluted Earth.

The past years, however, have not been all peaceful in space. Trouble soon broke out between the colonies, and war threatened to disrupt the new world. This led to the Gundam Fight being established.

To prevent further bloodshed, the quad-rennial Gundam Fight pitches colony against colony in a mobile suit proxy war that, using the entire Earth as the ring, decides which nation will rule the Earth Sphere for four years. G Gundam opens at the start of the 13th Gundam Fight, to which Neo Hong Kong enters as the reigning champion.

Main Characters

Neo Japan
Domon Kasshu, Rain Mikamura, Doctor Mikamura, Urube Ishikawa, Doctor Ka
Prime Minister Karato

Gundam Fighters from Other Countries
Chibodee Crocket, Sai Saishi, George De Sand, Argo Gulskii, Allenby Beardsley, Mic
Chariot, Gentle Chapman, Master Asia

Devil Gundam Force
Kyoji Kasshu

Main Mecha

Neo Japan
Shining Gundam, Burning Gundam, Rising Gundam

Gundam Fighters from Other Countries
Gundam Maxter (Neo America), Dragon Gundam (Neo China), Gundam Rose (
France), Mobile Fighter Mirage Gundam (Neo France), Bolt Gundam (Neo Rus
Shadow Gundam (Neo Germany), Haow Gundam (Neo Hong Kong), Noble Gun
(Neo Sweden)

Survival Eleven
Neros Gundam (Neo Italy), Arachno Gundam (Neo Cuba), Spike Gundam (Neo Mex
Grizzly Gundam (Neo Canada), Royal Gundam (Neo England), Gundam Scimitar (
Turkey), Mummy Gundam XIII (Neo Egypt), Mummy Gundam IV (Neo Egypt), Te
Gundam (Neo Mongolia), Gundam Magnat (Neo Poland)

League Finals
Zeus Gundam (Neo Greece), Toro Gundam (Neo Spain), Hurricane Gundam (Neo Holland), 7
Gundam (Neo Kenya), Cobra Gundam (Neo India), Mandala Gundam (Neo Nepal), Ashura Gun
(Neo Singapore), Skull Gundam (Neo Malaysia), Viking Gundam (Neo Norway), Jester Gun
(Neo Portugal), Mermaid Gundam (Neo Denmark)

Shuffle Alliance
Mobile Fighter Shuffle Joker, Mobile Fighter Shuffle Diamond, Mobile Fighter Sh
Club, Mobile Fighter Shuffle Spade

Devil Gundam Force
Devil Gundam (Neo Japan), Master Gundam (Neo Hong Kong), Mobile Horse Fuun
(Neo Hong Kong), Mobile Fighter Walter Gundam, Mobile Fighter Grand Gund
Mobile Fighter Raven Gundam, Mobile Suit Dark Army

What is the Gundam Fight? 11

E ven after the advent of the colonies, mankind continues to wage war. However, major advances have been made in weapon technology, and each conflict brings the human race closer to its own destruction.

As a result of this repeated warfare and mass slaughter, mankind finally sets about considering a new system that will allow states to battle it out without risking their own annihilation. The answer is the Gundam Fight.

Simply put, a Gundam Fight pits one Gundam against another in a tournament that decides which nation shall rule the colonies for the next four years. Each nation has its respective Gundam, and the last mobile suit left standing is the winner.

Theoretically, Gundam Fights are highly refined proxy wars fought by Gundams on behalf of the various nation states to prevent mass destruction and indiscriminate killing.

However, the selected fight ring is none

other than the earth. Earth-bound people, those which have not migrated into space, get caught up in the fighting. It is this contradiction that is the central theme of the series.

For a nation state to participate in a Gundam Fight, it has to have acquired sufficient technological know-how to enable it to develop a Gundam that stands a chance of winning. It must also have accomplished pilots with the skills necessary to operate a Gundam.

From our world view, Gundam Fights are akin to the sport of F-1 motor racing, where victory depends on a combination of first-class drivers, mechanics and machines.

Seven basic rules, laid down in an international treaty, govern a Gundam Fight. Each participating colony is expected to adhere strictly to these rules.

Model: MG GF13-017NJII God Gundam
Scale: 1/100
Built by RUN

International Rules

1. Any Gundam whose head is destroyed is disqualified.
   (Supplement to Article 1: Killing and wounding caused in error during competition is permissible.)
2. It is forbidden to target the cockpit of an opponent.
3. Gundams damaged on any part of the body except the head may be repaired as often as is necessary and continue to compete.
4. Gundam fighters must assume responsibility for the protection of their Gundams at all times.
5. All battles shall be conducted one-on-one.
6. The Gundam fighter is the representative of his or her nation. He/she must do nothing to lower the prestige of, or dishonor, that nation.
7. The fight ring is Earth.
   (Supplement to Article 7: Gundam fighters will not be prosecuted for destroying buildings on Earth during the competition.)

See questions

17 50

MSGeans...

What does Char wear on his days off? According to one Tokyo company, the answer may be as prosaic as a pair of jeans. In May of 2003, Yen Jeans released a limited line of denims under the label Char's Jeans. However, not one pair ever sat for more than a few minutes on a store shelf. This being Tokyo, the entire shipment had been snapped up in advance by a horde of mostly 30-ish young men, the same generation that had been spoon-fed Mobile Suit Gundam as kids.

But why Char's Jeans? Well, according to the maker, Char, the revengeful loner, and Yen Jeans, the designer brand that shies away from mass-production, are both unique characters - enigmatic; remote; cryptic, if you like. Mmm...

True, there is only one Char. However, there are some 1,200 pairs of his jeans walking around Japan, and in no less than four different styles. Still, if Char has managed to get his hands on a pair, he probably had to wipe out a few fans to do it.

Char's MS mark stitched onto the pocket.

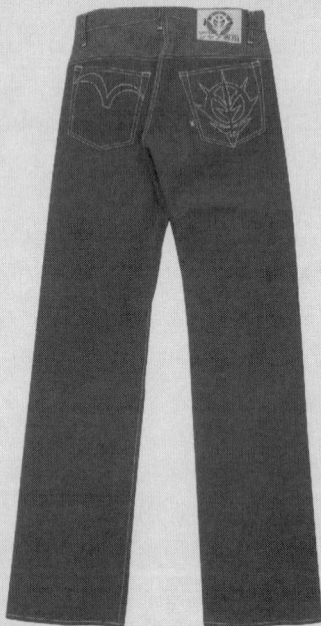
Char's Jeans
Type A (803-CA) 12-ounce denim in Char's trademark red and off-pink.
Stone-washed: US$300 Ordinary: US$200
Type B (110-CA) 14-ounce denim in blue with Char-red stitching.
Stone-washed: US$330 Ordinary: US$230

What is the Mobile Trace System? 12

I n the world of G Gundam, the cockpits from which the Gundams are controlled are based on a common standard, which adopts a technology called the Mobile Trace System.

This is composed of a membrane made up of unlimited nano-machines that envelop the body of the fighter pilot, allowing him to replicate his own movements through the larger medium of the Gundam.

This, therefore, synchronizes the movements of the fighter and the Gundam, allowing man and machine to act in total unison. However, another feature of this system is that damage to the Gundam is relayed to the fighter.

To skillfully pilot a Gundam and rise to the top of the Gundam fighting world, it is not only necessary to be trained in the mechanical basics of Gundam control, but also to hone the body and sharpen one's reflexes.

The scenes of Domon learning self-defense and undergoing special training are

See questions
17 18 20 50

included to illustrate how the Mobile Trace System operates.

Model: MG GF13-001NHII Master Gundam
Scale: 1/100
Built by RUN

Who or what is the Devil Gundam that Domon is searching for?

13

I t is the year FC 59. In Neo Japan, Doctor Kasshu, the father of the lead character Domon, and his son Kyoji, elder brother of Domon, have succeeded in developing Ultimate Gundam.

However, Neo Japan's military seizes Ultimate Gundam after false intelligence indicates father and son plan to use it to undermine order in the colonies.

In response, Kyoji activates Ultimate Gundam and, after battling the Neo Japan forces, escapes to Earth, where he crash-lands after burning up when entering the atmosphere.

Ultimate Gundam is believed to be destroyed in the crash. However, this particular Gundam harbors secret powers - the capabilities associated with the Three Great Theories of Self-regeneration, Self-propagation and Self-evolution.

Therefore, even if totally destroyed, Ultimate Gundam can reproduce itself via its

See Glossary
FC
Ultimate Gundam

self-regeneration function. It is because of this awesome power that Ultimate Gundam becomes known in time as Devil Gundam.

Also, based on these self-regeneration capabilities, it becomes evident that Devil Gundam will eventually be fully restored, and that Kyoji will be free to carry out a reign of destruction. It is projected that it will take one year for Devil Gundam to fully restore the damage caused on entry into the earth's atmosphere.

Earth, at the time, is under the control of Neo Hong Kong, meaning the Neo Japan military is unable to intervene. Its only chance is the 13th Gundam Fight, which is scheduled to be held one year later, in FC 60, and will again put the control of space at stake.

Neo Japan's leaders realize that by having the earth the ring for the Gundam Fight will allow their forces to move freely on the planet, regardless of who is in control.

Neo Japan nominates Domon Kasshu, the elder brother of Kyoji and son of Doctor Kasshu, to contest the Gundam Fight. Domon is the martial arts master of the colonies, and fights under the nom de guerre King of Hearts.

The Neo Japan forces order Domon to overthrow Devil Gundam and emerge victorious from the tournament.

See questions
14 15 17 18
20

What are DG Cells?

14

D G is short for "Devil Gundam." Being composed of DG Cells, Devil Gundam is endowed with the qualities of self-regeneration, self-propagation and self-evolution. The cells are, in fact, microscopic nanomachines that can function as a kind of biomechanical virus.

Humans can be infected by DG Cells by coming into contact with Devil Gundam. Infection causes the body to grow metalic scales, especially around the area of the wound. Infected humans can then be controlled by Devil Gundam itself.

Because the cells contain self-regeneration qualities, they can regenerate dead flesh, bringing corpses back to life. When the cells infect machines, such as Gundams, the machines not only take on new formats, but also experience huge increases in power.

See questions
13 15

D evil Gundam is composed of DG Cells, which were originally developed in order to regenerate Planet Earth. Hence, Devil Gundam has been input with a program designed to revitalize.

However, this program goes into automatic reset due to the shock experienced when entering the earth's atmosphere, causing the data to be lost.

What probably happens next is that Devil Gundam reinterprets the principals of Earth regeneration implanted in his memory and concludes that he must destroy mankind. Devil Gundam's new principals of conduct are that in order to revitalize the planet, he must exterminate all humans.

Moreover, during reconstitution following entry into the earth's atmosphere, the anger of Kyoji over the death of his mother is read into the memory of Devil Gundam, working to increase the intensity of his rage. As a result, he becomes an extremely dangerous entity.

See questions
13 14

Why is Master Asia able to pilot a Gundam without wearing a fighting suit? 16

The Mobile Trace System employed in G Gundam allows mobile suits (known as Mobile Fighters) to be operated by relaying the will, through motions, of the pilot, or Gundam Fighter, to the system. Damage, however, suffered by the machine is relayed back to the man.

The fighting suit, which most G Fighters wear, monitors the pilot's motions so that they can be replicated by his Mobile Fighter.

However, Master Asia, with is highly conditioned body and mind, appears strong enough to operate a Mobile Fighter with his bare hands, and is able to dispense with the fighting suit.

Or so it appears...

However, according to the director of the series, Yasuhiro Imamura, the main reason for not putting Master Asia and the members of the Shuffle Alliance into fighting suits was that they just didn't look good in them. Imamura-san sent down the order - "Leave him just as he is!", and that's basically all there is to know.

See Glossary
Gundam Fighter
Mobile Fighter
Shuffle Alliance

See questions
12 15 17

Gundam Goes Postal

Between 1999 and 2001, Japan's postal service released a series of stamp sets that commemorated a century of cultural landmarks. The 15th edition, which went on sale in October 2000, featured nine musical and television highlights from the years 1975 to 1983.

It is an incongruous collection. Recognition of the karaoke and electronic music booms of the period is justifiable, as perhaps is homage to Oshin, the hit drama that attracted addled fans Asiawide. However, the inclusion of UFO, the smash hit by '70s duo Pink Lady, suggests somebody down at the post office has licked one too many stamps.

This obvious lapse of sanity is fortunately remedied by the fact that not one, but two of the 10 stamps in this set represent the biggest cultural gun of the era, Mobile Suit Gundam. And if that's not enough, and for many it wasn't, as this particular edition is now a coveted collector's item, the illustrated margin depicts a host of Gundam characters nonchalantly posing for a family photo.

Certainly, it could be argued that Pink Lady's mailing power, at the letter-standard 80 yen, easily outguns MSG's meagre 50 yen denomination, enough only for a domestic postcard. But that ignores the very real possibilty of philatelic fusion, unleashing a postalactic energy that would bring the coast of North America and the capitals of Europe into range. Just imagine the headlines: Gundam Goes Postal!

Price Wars: This set is now worth a lot more than 740 yen.

Why does Domon clash with his mentor Master Asia? 17

Master Asia and Domon are teacher and pupil who eventually come to blows over their conflicting interests in Devil Gundam.

Master Asia is truly concerned about the environment of Planet Earth, and believes Gundam Fights, which are fought out on Earth, are responsible for much of the damage that exists there.

As a result, he decides that in order to revive the planet, it is necessary to annihilate mankind. The most effective way to achieve this, he believes, is to use Devil Gundam.

Domon, on the other hand, has come to Earth to secretly recover Devil Gundam in order to have his father released from the sentence of eternal freezing that has been imposed upon him.

Therefore, it isn't difficult to understand how master and pupil arrive at opposing points of view, and how a clash between them becomes inevitable.

However, their differences are not borne out of feelings of hatred, and deep down the master and pupil relationship lives on. Proof, if need be, can be found in the fact that Master Asia instructs Domon in the secrets of a new martial art - Sekiha Tenkyoken.

Their confrontation is one between teacher and pupil forced by the tragedy of fate.

See questions

11 13 15 16
18 20

Why is Doctor Kasshu, father of Domon and Kyoji, sentenced to eternal freezing? 18

Ultimate Gundam is designed by Domon's father, Doctor Kasshu, and his elder brother, Kyoji, for the purpose of revitalizing Earth.

However, this fuels the envy of Doctor Mikamura, a rival scientist who desperately wants to make the theories expounded by Doctor Kasshu his own. Mikamura's obsessive jealousy goes out of control when he is eventually shown the completed Ultimate Gundam.

Meanwhile, the military's Major Urube has also zeroed in on the overwhelming power of Ultimate Gundam. Along with Mikamura and the police, Urube turns up at Kasshu's lab, intent on confiscating Ultimate Gundam.

Kyoji, however, finds out what's going on and escapes to Earth with Ultimate Gundam. Having failed in their mission, Urube and Mikamura concoct a report that they present to the government of Neo Japan. In it, they claim that Kyoji's aim is to use Ultimate Gundam to conquer all space.

See Glossary
Ultimate Gundam

As a result, Doctor Kasshu is charged with treason as an accomplice and sentenced to eternal freezing, though this is simply a ruse to silence him. In exchange for the release of his father, Domon agrees to participate in a Gundam Fight.

See questions 13 17 20

What are Shining Gundam's special features? 19

Shining Gundam is designed by Doctor Kasshu's friend and rival, Doctor Mikamura, to be Neo Japan's Mobile Fighter for the important 13th Gundam Fight.

Doctor Mikamura has successfully applied the theories of the revolutionary Emotional Energy System to Mobile Fighters, and this is the system adopted by Shining Gundam.

Why the system is so radically different is that it manages to convert the heightened emotions of the Gundam Fighters into energy. It can also activate this increased energy in such hyper modes as the Shining Finger Sword.

The Gundam Fighter who most effectively harnesses this anger-based energy is Domon, which is one reason why he is picked to participate in the 13th Gundam Fight.

See Glossary

Shining Gundam
Mobile Fighter
Gundam Fighter

See questions

11 13 17 18 20

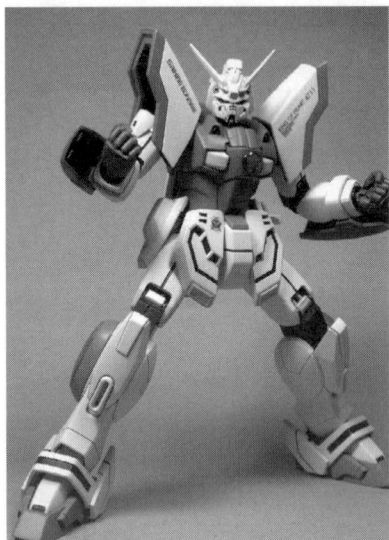

Model: MG GF13-017NJ Shining Gundam
Scale: 1/100
Built by RUN

Is it true that Doctor Mikamura considers Domon to be little more than a guinea pig?

20

The Shining Gundam piloted by Domon emerges as a wreck from the 11-month elimination phase known as Survival Eleven, leading to the development of a successor - God Gundam.

Even in normal mode, God Gundam has an in-built mental and physical Mobile Trace System that far exceeds the hyper mode of Shining Gundam.

This part of the story is based on the belief that Doctor Mikamura has been using Domon as a human guinea pig who looks destined to die as the system eats away at his body and mind.

However, the director realized that if he pursued this storyline, God Gundam and Doctor Mikamura would end up as villains, and somewhere along the line he decided to change course. As a result, Domon's capabilities, which come to the fore when he first pilots God Gundam, eventually eclipse those of Shining Gundam.

See Glossary

Shining Gundam
Survival Eleven
God Gundam

See questions

12 13 19 51

Gundam File 005

Fight and Die (well, almost...) for the Federation!

It's one thing watching Gundam. It's a different thing altogether actually being part of it! And now you can.

That's if you reserve your seat at Fujikyu Highland's simulated GUNDAM THE RIDE.

Here's how it goes. It's UC 79, and the Earth Federation and the Principality of Zeon are slugging it out. You're aboard a Federation ship heading for the Side 6 space colony. You're a civilian and have little to do with the war, when suddenly - BANG! - the final battle comes knocking and the fun begins.

GUNDAM THE RIDE is quite a feat of technology in itself. The graphics are the product of Gundam anime creators, the MMM60 simulator is the very same one used to train 747 pilots, eight huge speakers rock the small auditorium, and each seat is fitted with a device known as a Winble, which reacts with jerks and spasms to every sudden shift in the unfolding battle.

Fortunately, your character survives with little more than a racing heartbeat and a stupid grin.

Keep it real! A 33-foot Gundam is the entrance to GUNDAM THE RIDE.
Fujikyu Highland -
http://www.fujikyu.co.jp/

Who or what is Schubertz Bruder? 21

Schubertz Bruder is the Neo German Gundam Fighter. He employs an art called "German Ninjutsu", thought to have derived from ancient Japanese ninjutsu. The mask that he usually wears gives him an air of mystery.

He emerges to help Domon at every step along the way, eventually guiding him to victory. In Giana, where he undertakes his training, Schubertz initiates Domon in the ways of Meikyou Shisui - the art of destroying one's illusions. It is because Domon masters this ascetic that he is able to activate the hyper mode when piloting Shining Gundam.

However, the true identity of Schubertz Bruder, who has so far acted almost as an elder brother to Domon, is Kyoji, Domon's actual elder brother, albeit in android form.

In the end, Domon destroys Schubertz Bruder using Sekiha Tenkyoken he has learned from Master Asia.

See Glossary

Gundam Fighter
Meikyou Shisui
Shining Gundam

See questions

13 17 18 20

Gundam File 006

Gundam Bottle Caps

In Japan, giveaways are nothing new. Drinks and candies often come with little extras attached. Stickers, CDs, chocolate eggs, toys - these freebies, known as *shokugan* in Japanese, now fuel a $500 million business.

Small models of extinct animals are popular, as are characters from Japanese anime and Disney. But there's a ton of other stuff just waiting to be had by the lucky consumer.

And from September 2003, for a limited period only, it was Gundam's turn to get in on the action. With every 500 ml aluminum bottle of Pespi Cola came one of 32 characters or mecha from Mobile Suit Gundam in the form of a bottle cap.

The line-up was remarkably extensive and each model, although no larger than a thumb, surprisingly detailed. Collectors got to wage cola-cap wars between Amuro Ray and Sayla Mass on one side, and a plethora of baddies, such as Ramba Ral, Gelgoog, Zock and the inimitable Char, on the other.

It was a soda success story, with even non-Pepsi drinkers snapping up the models while they lasted. 24-hour convenience stores, in particular, attracted throngs of Gundam fans well after the malls had closed.

This was a boom. And, naturally, things got a bit crazy. Not knowing which character was hiding in the sealed wrapper meant that many fans ended up with the same bottle cap over and over again. And this meant yet another trip to the store.

Not surprisingly, some people started buying 24-bottle cases just to get at the Gundam goodies inside. And what made this craze all the more exciting, and frustrating, was that two of the 32 giveaways were listed simply as "Secret I" and "Secret II".

The craze eventually passed, as they always do. But its legend lingers on. Most homes throughout Japan can boast at least one Gundam bottle cap, and the Internet is awash with collectors trying to get their hands on that one last character to complete the series.

But did anyone ever discover what Secrets I and II actually were?

Pepsi's Gundam bottle caps, They look good on Coke bottles too...

Is it true that Japanese fans of the original Gundam didn't like G Gundam when it was released? 22

Mobile Fighter G Gundam was created to celebrate the 15th anniversary of the first Gundam series, and introduces Future Century, an altogether different era to the Universal Century of the previous series.

Part of the reason for the creation of this new era is that the original Gundam had become bogged down in scientific explanations, making the story overly detailed and complicated.

The newer G Gundam aimed to reproduce the kind of robot animation that existed before Gundam - the simple fun of good and bad robots slugging it out in space.

However, the reaction of anyone who had faithfully followed the previous Gundam series may have been, "This is a totally different cosmology." And it was because of this new world that G Gundam didn't immediately catch on.

For hard-core fans, the idea of having Gundams face off must have come as quite a

See Glossary
Universal Century

79

shock.

Still, the relatively simple concept behind the new series - introducing many new Gundams and having them fight each other - gained a following among the very robot anime fans who had previously avoided Gundam because of its overly complicated plot.

Furthermore, although superficially the show is simpler, the plot is, in fact, considerably complex. This eventually convinced fans of the original Gundam of its authenticity, and it became a big hit in Japan, and even bigger in the US.

This newfound popularity of a very different Gundam opened the door to such series as Mobile Suit Gundam Wing and Mobile Suit Gundam SEED.

The radical changes in G Gundam were also a result of surveys conducted into the type of images popular in Japanese animation.

The images of Mobile Suit Gundam Wing and Mobile Suit Gundam SEED are also different, again the result of employing images prevalent to the moment in an attempt to carve out a new fan base, rather than merely maintain a standard feel throughout the series.

The success of G Gundam has proved to be a major influence on the entire Gundam series.

See questions
10 23 38 50
51 52

Mobile Suit Gundam Wing

Broadcast from April 7, 1995 to March 29, 1996.

Overview

Mobile Suit Gundam Wing is the second part of the new Gundam series. In continuing the pattern set by G Gundam of introducing a variety of new and increasingly more complicated Gundam characters, Gundam W follows the previous series, which moved away from the concepts that made up the Universal Century. At the same time, however, Gundam W was also created with the original story line of the Gundam series in mind. The series was popular with female fans, introducing many characters, such as the five handsome main characters, who would have seemed out of place in previous series.

Story

The year is AC 195. In opposition to the Earth Federation, which is attempting to unify the space migrants by force of arms, each colony looks to develop high-capabilty mobile suits - Gundams - as a symbol of their will to resist.

These five Gundams, and the pilots who operate them, descend to earth. Under Operation Meteor, their mission is to destroy the base of the secret military society OZ, which is backing the Federation.

At the same time, Relena Darlian, whose life becomes threatened by one of the pilots, Heero Yuy, embarks on a fateful adventure.

Main Characters

Gundams
Heero Yuy, Duo Maxwell, Trowa Barton, Quatre Raberba Winner, Chang Wufei

OZ
Zechs Merquise, Lucrezia Noin, Treize Kushrenada, Lady Une

Allies
Relena Darlian, The Gundam Developers, Sally Po, Catherine Bloom, Howard, Maganac Corps

Main Mecha

Gundams
XXXG-01W Wing Gundam, XXXG-01D Gundam Deathsythe, XXXG-01H Gundam Heavyarms, XXXG-01SR Gundam Sandrock, XXXG-01S Shenlong Gundam, XXXG-00W0 Wing Gundam Zero, XXXG-01D2 Gundam Deathsythe H, XXXG-01S2 Altron Gundam

OZ
OZ-00MS Tallgeese, OZ-06MS Leo, OZ-07AMS Aries, OZ-07MS Tragos, OZ-08MMS Cancer, OZ-09MMS Pisces, OZ-12SMS Taurus, OZ-13MSX1 Vayeate, OZ-13MSX2 Mercurius, OZ-13MS Epyon

Allies
WMS-03 Maganac

Main Vehicles

Gundams
Peace Million

OZ
Space Fortress Barge

What kind of era is the After Colony of Mobile Suit Gundam Wing?

23

Mankind has grown tired of the continual disputes that plague Planet Earth. Setting his hopes on developing other worlds, man declares a momentous move into space - Year 1 of the After Colony.

However, along with the uninviting environments and new epidemics that this bold venture must overcome, the disputes between the various nations of Earth spill over into the colonies. These lead to armed clashes, and by AC 50 the earth is looking to curtail space migration.

While this is taking place, the Middle East nations, which have abandoned oil production, turn their attentions to space, looking to participate in the migration program. Using the diplomatic routes established during their years as oil producers, they succeed in alleviating the lack of resources that is the cause of many of the disputes by transporting a raw materials satellite into space. This eventually brings an end to conflicts, putting colonization plans back on track.

In AC 102, a century after the start of the new era, the first permanent colony, L1 - Lagrange point 1 - is completed, setting off a rush to develop Lagrange point colony clusters.

As international disputes escalate on Earth, a growing number of people flee into space. This triggers a decline in the earth's population.

As a result, in AC 133, the nations of the earth establish the United Earth Sphere Alliance. As well as bringing an end to disputes, the Alliance presses the colonies to join it.

See Glossary

Lagrange Points
United Earth Sphere
Alliance

Model: HG XXXG-01W Wing Gundam
Scale: 1/100
Built by AKM

Persuasion is backed by overwhelming military might.

The colonies establish an autonomous government in AC 139 in an attempt to shake off interference from Planet Earth, but fail in the face of the military muscle of the Alliance and are forced to relinquish power in AC 140.

By the mid-140s, the Alliance is wielding its power to bring the colonies under military control in order to snuff out the radical activities of independence agitators. It soon decides on an open-ended military presence.

Against this background of opposition to the Alliance, a colony conference is established in AC 150. Heero Yuy is elected representative in AC 165, and he consistently promotes non-violence and de-militarization.

Following the proclamation of de-militarization in AC 173, Heero Yuy is within a whisker of seeing it adopted in AC 175 by all nations, including those on Earth. However, he is assassinated by the secret society OZ, set up in AC 175 by the Romefeller Foundation, which views the course of events with little sympathy.

After Heero Yuy's death, the colonies fall into a state of chaos. The United Earth Sphere Alliance recovers the power lost under Heero Yuy's leadership and, using the pretext of maintaining law and order, dispatches the Specials - a new set of military mobile suits. This severs communication between the colonies, preventing new alliances.

Time passes, and in AC 195, in trying to bring an end to the war initiated by the Gundams sent to Earth by the anti-alliance colonist forces, the colonists propose the establishment of the United Earth Sphere State. The nations of the earth fall into line, and disputes finally end on Earth and in space.

See Glossary

Specials

See questions

24 25 30 50

What sort of activities is the Romefeller Foundation involved in? 24

The Romefeller Foundation was established by the monarchy and nobility, and is a veritable "Merchant of Death".

The Foundation largely funds the Alliance, and effectively controls it. The Foundation also successfully transfers the technology used in the mobile suits, originally intended as work machines, to military use, developing the major fighters of the Alliance, Leo and Aries.

Using these mobile suits, a unit called the Specials is established within the Alliance military, which becomes the de facto rulers of Earth once OZ seizes its chance and conquers the planet.

After setting in motion the invasion of space, the Foundation develops the Mobile Doll System. The effectiveness of the Mobile Dolls as powerful fighters soon becomes evident, leading the Foundation to begin mass production of the Dolls.

However, Treize Khushrenada, the commander of the Specials and an expounder of

See Glossary

United Earth Sphere
Alliance
Leo
Aries
Specials

89

man-to-man fighting, is against this. As a result, he is condemned to solitary confinement.

Meanwhile, OZ splits into two. The Foundation seizes on this as a chance to exterminate every last member of Treize's clique, and puts Operation Nova into action to conquer the earth.

With the success of Operation Nova, the Foundation brings most of Earth under its control. But the overwhelming military force with which it accomplishes this goal provokes opposition by the world's nations, inexorably drawing support for the Sanc Kingdom.

This forces the Foundation to attack and destroy the Sanc Kingdom. Duke Dermail hopes to utilize Relena's popularity and appoints her as representative after she has surrendered. However, Relena's pacifism wins the approval and support of the Foundation's board, and as a result, it makes peace overtures.

The White Fang uprising leads to a heightened sense of crisis among the senior members of the Foundation. They approve the appointment of Treize as representative, tilting the balance back towards militarization.

See Glossary

Treize Clique
Operation Nova
Sanc Kingdom

See questions

25 26 33 50

What is OZ?

25

O Z is a secret society founded in AC 175 as an advance guard of the Romefeller Foundation. It is responsible for the assassination of Heero Yuy in the same year.

OZ also embarks on the military application of the mobile suits, successfully developing the Tallgeese. The society goes on to develop Leo and Aries using the same technology.

Expanding its power while keeping its existence a secret, OZ also establishes the fighting unit the "Specials," based on the mobile suits, within the military.

In AC 195, as the invasion of the Gundams sends tremors through the universe, OZ releases Operation Daybreak - a coup d'etat - annihilating the Earth Sphere United Nation.

OZ advances into space, after taking over the earth, but a dispute arises between the Romefeller Foundation and Treize Khushrenada concerning the Mobile Doll System, which has been put into combat use. Treize is stripped of his command and placed in solitary confine-

See Glossary

Tallgeese
Leo
Aries
Specials
Operation Daybreak
Earth Sphere United Nation

ment.

This leads to a fateful division, and the OZ/Treize clique and the Romefeller Foundation eventually clash.

See Glossary

Treize Clique

See questions

24 26 30

Model: HG XXXG-00W0 Wing Gundam Zero
Scale: 1/100
Built by AKM

What is the Mobile Doll System? 26

The "Doll" of Mobile Doll System stands for "Direct Operational Led Labor". Developed by chief engineer Tsubarov of the Romefeller Foundation, the original idea comes from the five engineers responsible for the development of Tallgeese.

Tallgeese, they discover, is too powerful for any human to operate. This leads the engineers to develop the Zero System by which to strengthen the functional capabilities of human beings.

However, one other option is to remove the living organism - the pilot - from the mobile suit. This automatic piloting system becomes known as the Mobile Doll System.

The Mobile Doll System does not require any pilot skills and exhibits no human-attributed fatigue or error. Moreover, reaction speed and flexibility far exceeds that of manned machines.

The Mobile Doll at first appears the ideal fighting system. However, the untrammeled

See Glossary
Tallgeese

slaughter it results in threatens unprecedented tragedy, one reason why Treize Khushrenada, the OZ commander, is so opposed to it.

See questions
24 27 50

Model:B Club XXXG-01SR Gundam Sandrock
Scale: 1/100
Built by AKM

What is the Zero System?   27

A cockpit system mounted on Wing Gundam Zero and Gundam Epyon, its official title is Zoning and Emotional Range Omitted System.

Engineers believe they have created the ultimate in mobile suit capabilities with the development of Tallgeese. The Zero System is developed to resolve the one problem - that no humans are able to pilot Tallgeese.

The Zero System works on the integration of the pilot's brain waves with the actual mobile suit. All information detected by the system's sensors is immediately transmitted to the pilot's brain, bypassing the normal human receptors. Furthermore, any thoughts that the pilot has are detected by the system, which then analyzes and acts upon them. With the Zero System, it is possible to control a mobile suit with one's brain much like controlling one's own body. This gives Tallgeese a murderous advantage over other mobile suits.

In battle situations, the system is able to

See Glossary

Wing Gundam Zero
Tallgeese

calculate the state of the fight, feeding back a vast amount of data to the pilot, including forecasts. Therefore, in a way, the system is able to read the future.

However, these forecasts can include information concerning the death of the pilot, which can lead to an emotional over-reaction in the face of such dire prospects. Therefore, it is crucial that the pilot is extremely strong-willed. There are also cases of emotional surges or hallucinations due to the impact of the system on brain cells.

See questions

26 50

What is Gundanium Alloy? 28

Gundanium Alloy stands for "Generic on Universal Neutrally Different Alloy"; a group of alloys that can only be produced in the zero-gravity conditions of space.

By altering their sequences, structures and charges, the alloys can be made to absorb and disrupt all kinds of magnetic waves, as well as alter their high-temperature resilience and anti-corrosive qualities.

Also, using these alloys, it has been possible to confirm such attributes as the damping, offsetting and phase-transfer in surface change initiated by metal-reactive plasma and electrically charged particles. As such, this is the "dream material" for mobile suits.

However, it is still difficult to forecast any cost-reductions based on mass production or an end to low productivity. Also, because there has been little need for such high-performance material so far, the alloy has yet to be put into common use. The Alliance's weapons are almost all made of titanium-based alloys.

See Glossary

United Earth Sphere Alliance

See questions

50

Gundam File   007

Catwalk Gundam

It's not only Gundamaniacs who've gotta have it all! Anime fans of all stripes collect anime merchandise of every shape and size. That's just the way the world is. However, there are some, and increasingly many more, that don't simply want to collect their favorite character's goods, they WANT TO BE their favorite character. Enter cosplay. Once the redoubt of giggly Japanese girls, the surreal culture of dressing up in anime couture is now the bane of parents across North America.

Lalah Sune, Sayla Mass, Fraw Bow and Amuro Ray from Mobile Suit Gundam. First MSG just won't go away.

ZAFT Pilots Nical Amarfi and Yzak Jule from MSG SEED. Now where did we leave our mobile suits...

What is Operation Meteor? 29

Operation Meteor is the name given to a plan devised by the residents of the colonies, who, opposed to the Alliance, intend to send the Gundams to Earth disguised as meteors.

The operation takes place on April 7, AC 195, 20 years after the assassination of Heero Yuy. It originally calls for the Gundams to take over Earth amid the confusion that is expected to take place in the wake of their arrival.

However, the operation doesn't go according to plan due to disagreement among the colony clusters. Those opposed to such "nefarious tactics" set in motion the secret mission to destroy the society OZ using the five Gundams.

See Glossary

United Earth Sphere Alliance

See questions

30

Gundam Fortune-telling?

Few anime-lovers know of a mini-boom that has been shaping the world of Gundamaniacs of late.

"Gundam fortune-telling," as it's simply translated, is a rather suspect science that grew out of the "animal fortune-telling" fad popular in Japan some years ago. In the bestial version, individuals were ascribed certain animal traits depending on their date of birth. This gave rise to an extraordinary state of affairs in which the most banal middle-aged salary men began describing themselves as black panthers, monkeys or worse.

One thing led to another, and somewhere along the way the animals were exchanged for Gundam mecha. Based on date of birth and blood type, with this new method it was again possible to tell someone's character traits. However, divination was made through one of 48 Mobile Suits and Mobile Armor from the Universal Century. It wasn't long before people were being greeted with such inquiries as, "Are you one of the Zeon Forces or part of the Federation?"

It only remains to say that hot on the heels of this rather odd craze came the merchandising... Believe it or not, 48 corresponding fortune-telling Gundams, overridingly cute in design, are now sold throughout this great nation.

Ugh?! Mobile Fortune
Gundam - $3.20 each

Is the pilot of Wing Gundam and the pacifist leader Heero Yuy the same person? **30**

The truth is that two characters with exactly the same name appear in the Gundam series. One of them is the pilot of Wing Gundam and hero of the series.

The other is the charismatic pacifist leader Heero Yuy, who preaches de-militarization and persuades the Alliance to grant autonomy to the colonies. This Yuy is assassinated in AC 175 by OZ, the secret society that has little love of pacifists.

See Glossary

Wing Gundam
United Earth Sphere Alliance

See questions

23 25 29

The Girls of Gundam Wing

Gundam has a plethora of girl characters, all of whom suffer from both perfection and absurdity. This is no more truer than in Gundam Wing, where wacky women are everywhere, battling enemies, leading revolutions, ruling countries, and falling for one gorgeous space cowboy after another.

GW kick-ass femininity is perhaps best personified in the character of OZ officer Lucrezia Noin, who has devoted herself to Zechs. Her costume is suggestive of the male roles in Japan's all-female cross-dressing theater, Takarazuka. As with Takarazuka, her gender-bender style has attracted a horde of adoring boy fans. However, she seems unaware - or unpreturbed - by this devotion, and loyally follows Zechs to his destiny.

Many girl fans fell for Noin when she humbly bowed to Zechs' demands to protect his sister, Relena, from the evil OZ. For her female admirers she encompasses all that is noble in men, and all that is beautiful in women. She has neither the impatience of Zechs or Wufei, nor the sangfroid of Lady Une and Treize. Noin is a rare breed; she is clearheaded and just, able to judge right from wrong.

Lady Une is a world unto herself. Two worlds, in fact. With her glasses on, she is a minipulative troublemaker. With them off, she becomes as sweet as pie. Lady Une is one of Gundam's most misunderstood characters. As Treize's senior adjutant she is feared by all. Her ruthless reputation preceeds her, and to many she is the epitome of villainy. But, as the series unfolds, we see another side to her peculiar personality. She is the true heart of OZ and the bane of all colonial resistance. She will do anything to serve her master, Treize, even suicide if so ordered. She is passionately devoted to her duty and to the man she loves.

Cathy, the circus knife-thrower, is a stubborn young lady indeed. Although Trowa insists otherwise, she sticks to the belief that he's her brother, and by doing so causes no end of trouble. When Duo turns up at the circus to persuade Trowa to return to being a pilot, Cathy's interference actually leads him to don his space suit and return to the life he thought he'd forgotten forever.

Sally Po is a quick-thinking resistance fighter with a penchant for peculiar hair styles and near-suicidal warfare. She is also known by fans as the only one who can put up with Wufei. The sight of the Gundams leaves her weak at the knees, and she quits OZ to start a new life with the boys. In many ways she is like a patroness, risking all to support the Gundam teams. Carreering her ship Peace Million into the enemy Libra in an attack that nearly cost the lives of herself and her crew was just one example of her die-hard attitude. Alas, she is another smitten by G-pilot charm.

Dorothy Catalonia is a war-crazed peacenik. She lives for

the day that peace will dawn, but is quite happy to spill a lot of blood along the way. She believes in war with honor, and idolizes such leaders as Relena and Zechs for their fearlessness and strength in battle. Flattery of others is another of her fatal flaws. With long flowing blonde hair, lavender eyes and unusual split eyebrows, Dorothy Catalonia has a commanding appearance. But she seems always to be playing someone else's sidekick.

As well as her remarkable eyebrows, which are a family trait, other noticable characteristics are her annoying laugh, her cynical smile and her uncontrollable glee when battle is about to commence. Many believe that she has a blood-lust, but nothing could be further from the truth. The death of her father in battle when she was young has left her with a fear of dying. Survival is her one true goal. To conquer death, she must fight, and this she does. But Dorothy is ridden with regrets. Her past still haunts her, causing her to commit stupid and sometimes murderous acts, such as joining with White Fang and even trying to kill Quatre Reberba Winner.

But of all Gundam's leading ladies, it is Relena who makes the least sense. Yes, she has a very important role to play, and thus has many adoring fans for whom she is a cool promoter of world peace. However, her stalking of Heero, the way she talks to him when he's not even there, the fact that she attempts to assassinate OZ operatives, and her scewered theories on paci-fism prove her to be remarkably unstable.

Her Gandhi-esque beliefs in world peace and non-violence are quickly discarded when the Gundam pilots smash their way in to save her from OZ fighters. She even dares Heero to come back and kill her and her brother Zechs simply because she wants to see him again. Following in her father's footsteps, she rebuilds the destroyed Sanc Kingdom, only to dismantle it once it proves to be a disadvantage to her. In the end, she even dumps the name Peacecraft and returns to Darlian without any prior announcement.

It's difficult to believe that anybody in their right mind would want to live in a place ruled by such a capricious young woman. But if we look at her brother Zechs we see the same unstable behavior, such as his attempt to destroy Earth, or when he renames himself Preventor Wind. It's obvious to any fan of Gundam that the Peacecraft family aren't playing with a full deck, and Relena, alongside her suicidal Heero, is the wildest card of them all.

Model: HG XXXG-01S Shenlong Gundam
Scale: 1/100
Built by AKM

What is the Terra-forming expounded by Relena?

31

As the name implies, Terra-forming is the process of recreating the earth's atmosphere on other planets. The process is already being considered as a future solution for when the earth's atmosphere will no longer be able to sustain human life.

In the case of Mars, making the climate suitable for human-beings is the first order, and is achieved by solving the problem of the cold climate of a planet further away from the sun than Earth.

This is done through the production and emission of chloro-flouro carbons, which have 10,000 times the green-house effect of carbon-dioxide, along with the green-house effect from carbon-dioxide existing in the planet's antartic pole and top-soil in the form of dry ice. Oceans are also produced by melting the subterranean ice. Resolving the problems of great temperature differences is done by the creation of clouds.

See Glossary
UC

See questions
32

Very Heavy Metal

If you think you've got every bit of Gundam merchandise that was ever made, then think again. Tokyo's Banpresto has taken Gundam's Beam Rifle and Zaku's Heat Hawk and remodeled them, of all things, into electric guitars!

Not only do they look cool, but the two very distinctive designs also come complete with in-built speakers, synthesized Gundam sounds, which, in the case of the Beam Rifle, are activated by squeezing on the guitar's trigger, and initialized straps and cases.

If you want to wake up the universe, or simply annoy your neighbors, then make the Gundam Sound Series your weapon of choice.

Gundam Grunge: Beam Rifle and Heat Hawk electric guitars ($850.00)
Strap: $55.00   Case: $85.00
http://www.banpresto.co.jp/

What is the true identity of the masked Zechs Merquise? 32

The masked man, Zechs Merquise, is a mobile suit pilot who seems to have been created with Char of the original Gundam series in mind.

Elder brother of Relena, his real name is Milliard Peacecraft. He infiltrates OZ in order to fully exact revenge for the destruction of the Sanc Kingdom. A skilful pilot, he is known as the "Lightning Count" for his exploits in the cockpit.

Zechs has the trust of his men, is a veteran fighter, and pilots a Tallgeese to counter the super-powerful capabilities of the Gundams.

However, having lost Otto Richter during the recapture of the Sanc Kingdom, and defeated General Daigo Onegel who destroyed Sanc, Zechs' will to continue battling weakens. He is particularly unhappy with the way OZ seems bent on merely creating one conflict after another. It is in his face-off with Heero Yuy that Zechs hopes to rediscover the fighting spirit.

However, in protecting Relena, Zechs dis-

See Glossary
Sanc Kingdom
Tallgeese

109

covers his true calling, and plunges, alone, into battle against the main force of the pursuing survey team. He's eventually forced to surrender, and is about to be brought before a court-martial when, once again, he is confronted by an overwhelming force, this time sent by Treize, who wants to see Zechs "die the death of a hero" as a way of underpinning the morale of OZ.

Zechs somehow manages to emerge victorious. Weakened, he is saved by Howard as he collapses. Howard sends him into space, where

Model: OZ-00MS Tallgeese
Scale: 1/100
Built by AKM

he attempts to halt the militarization of the colonies as the good-will ambassador of the Sanc Kingdom, but his mission is a failure. He is now going by his real name, Milliard Peacecraft

Zechs again sets out into space aboard Howard's Peace Million in an attempt to disrupt the Foundation's Operation Nova.

When he loses the Tallgeese in battle, Zechs obtains a Wing Gundam, and goes to the aid of the Sanc Kingdom, which is threatened with collapse in the face of an onslaught by the Foundation.

See Glossary

Operation Nova
Wing Gundam

But the Sanc Kingdom is destroyed by none other than Relena herself. Zechs has now all but lost the will to go on, but is forced into a final showdown with Heero, who attacks. Their Zero Systems both go out of control, resulting in neither being victorious. They then switch to Epyons.

Taking a break from fighting, Zechs is welcomed as a leader of White Fang by Quinze, and he pushes for the destruction of Earth. Zech's real intention is to do away with warfare by showing earthlings the futility of it all.

However, in his fight with Heero, he awakens to the fact that war cannot be fought with war, and instead volunteers to destroy the nuclear reactor powering the battleship Libra. Zechs disappears in the ensuing explosion.

See Glossary
Libra

See questions

5 25 27 30 31 33

What kind of organization is White Fang? **33**

White Fang is a revolutionary group, made up of civilians, that rises in armed rebellion against the control of OZ.

White Fang's origins are as a movement that began in the AC 140s to achieve self-rule for the colonies. The leaders were eventually labeled radicals by the Alliance and forced underground. The self-rule movement reaches its peak with the emergence of Heero Yuy, but is snuffed out following his assassination.

White Fang's effective leader is a man known as Quinze, who works for colonial self-rule alongside Heero Yuy, but becomes a fighter after his assassination. While engaged in acts of terror throughout the colonies, Quinze becomes involved in Operation Meteor.

However, due to opposition from pilots and engineers, Operation Meteor changes course. Quinze bides his time, and when the chance arises amid confusion at the Romefeller Foundation, he ropes in the Treize clique and

See Glossary

United Earth Sphere Alliance

Treize Clique

pushes White Fang to revolt.

White Fang begins by launching the Artemis Revolution, deemed a success with the capture of the OZ battleship Libra and the Lunar Base. Quinze uses his new strengths to destroy the OZ bases in each colony and, eventually, Space Fortress Barge.

See Glossary

Artemis Revolution
Libra
Lunar Base
Space Fortress Barge

See questions

24 25 29 30

Model: Gundam Wing Secret Five Mobil Suit
Scale: SD
Built by RUN

Why is it that Lady Une's character is so different according to whether she wears or removes her glasses? 34

L ady Une is the aide-de-camp to OZ commander Treize Khushrenada, and a woman who will stop at nothing to achieve her goals. The use of spectacles - which are really only fitted with ordinary glass - works to heighten her cruel image.

She implements numerous bold operations, such as the assassination of Darlian, the Alliance's Vice Minister for Foreign Affairs, when he visits the colonies, and the failed attempt to wipe out the Gundams in a nuclear explosion at their base.

She later becomes senior special assistant, responsible for the OZ space invasion, though shows a remarkably different side to her character in order to promote cooperation with the colonies.

It seems she possesses a split-personality, possibly born out of the stress she suffers due to her inability to undertsand the feelings that Treize has for her. As a result, she becomes aggressive when she wears the spectacles, and kindly and saint-like when she removes them.

Lady Une believes that by using the Mobile Dolls she will be able to finally possess Treize. However, once involved in the fight, she realizes finally how he feels about her. She manages to fuse her two personalities to fight for a future in which they will be together.

She revolts against the Romefeller Foundation in order to free the Gundam pilots and engineers held at Lunar Base, but is shot by Tsubarov and disappears.

When Space Fortress Barge falls, Lady Une is returned, unconscious, to Treize by Nicol and his cohorts. Awakening immediately before the battle, she saves Treize from the cannons of the Libra. However, because Wing Gundam is now badly damaged, they take control of the United Earth Sphere Alliance with the resources satellite MO2.

When the great war ends, she takes over the intelligence unit of the unified state, Preventer, under the code name Gold.

See Glossary

Lunar Base
Space Fortress Barge
Libra
Wing Gundam
United Earth Sphere Alliance
Resources Satellite MO2
Preventer

See questions

24 25 26

Is it true that in Japan Gundam Wing was particularly popular with girls? 35

Watching Gundam Wing, it seems that even from the production stage the series was designed with female viewers in mind. The choice of five handsome youths as main characters is all the proof you need.

The Gundam series was originally popular with teenage boys. But with G Gundam created 15 years after the first Gundam, the producers were looking to carve out a new fan base. They discovered that the scenes of Gundams battling each other appealed to viewers younger than previous fans, and thus G Gundam was created to include a lot of such action.

The producers then took this success and included all the elements they believed would appeal to girls. With Gundam Wing they succeeded, further spreading the popularity of the Gundam series.

See questions
10 22

Model: HG XXXG-01D Gundam Deathscythe
Scale: 1/100
Built by AKM

Model:B Club XXXG-01H Gundam Heavyarms
Scale: 1/100
Built by AKM

Mobile Suit Gundam SEED

Broadcast from October 5, 2002 to September 27, 2003.

Overview

23 years after MS Gundam, Mobile Suit Gundam SEED launches the series into the 21st century. The main character Kira Yamato and his old friend and antagonist Athrun Zara are forced into battle against each other.

Space warfare unfolds on an unprecedented scale, but battlegrounds shift from ground to sky to sea.

In having both the genetically enhanced Coordinators of ZAFT (Zodiac Alliance of Freedom Treaty) and the United Earth Sphere Alliance's Naturals fight it out, this series pursues the theme of whether human beings can go beyond race and religion to develop a truely universal understanding.

Story

It is Cosmic Era 70. The Bloody Valentine incident, sparked by friction between the Coordinators of ZAFT, a military force looking to establish its own economic zone, and the Naturals of the United Earth Sphere Alliance, becomes the catalyst for a full-fledged armed clash. The ZAFT forces use their MS to relentlessly overpower the UESA.

Kira Yamato is attending the industrial college on the resource satellite Heliopolos, part of the neutralist state Orb in L3. He's at his seminar, as usual, when he gets caught up in a ZAFT invasion, as its forces attempt to seize five recently completed new type mobile suit Gundams, one of which is a Strike Gundam, that have been secretly stored on the colony.

The surprise attack succeeds, and three of the five MS5 Gundams that the Alliance has secretly developed fall into the hands of ZAFT. A member of the ZAFT surprise attack team runs into Kira, and we realize it is his old friend Athrun Zara. The war eventually sees Kira climb into the cockpit of the Strike Gundam and Athrun into the other, and the two Gundams rise amid roaring flames...

Main Characters

United Earth Sphere Alliance
Kira Yamato, Murrue Ramus, Fllay Allster, Mwu La Fllaga, Miriallia Haww, Natarle Badgiruel, Kuzzey Buskirsk, Tolle Koenig, Ssigh Argyle, Dalida Loraha Chandra, Jackie Tonomura, Arnold Neumann, Romel Paru

ZAFT
Athrun (Aslan) Zara, Nical Amarfi, Yzak Jule, Dearka Elthman, Raww Le Klueze, Ades, Lacus Clyne, Miguel Aiman

The United Emirates of Orb
Caggali Yula Attha, Uzumi Nala Attha, Erica Simmons, Ledonil Kisaka, Mayura Lapats, Asagi Kodoueru, Julie Nien

Main Mecha

United Earth Sphere Alliance
GAT-X105 Strike Gundam, GAT-X370 Raider Gundam, GAT-X131 Calamity Gundam, ZGMF-X10A Freedom Gundam, GAT-01 Strike Dagger

ZAFT
GAT-X102 Duel Gundam, GAT-X103 Buster Gundam, GAT-X207 Blitz Gundam, GAT-X303 Aegis Gundam, AMF-101 DINN, ZGMF-1017 GINN, GMF-LRR704B GINN Reconnaissance Type, TFA-2 ZuOOT, TMF/A-803 LaGOWE, TMF/A-802 BuCUE, TMF/S-3 GINN OCHER, UMF-4A GOOhN, UMF-5 ZnO, ZGMF-515 CGUE, ZGMF-600 GuAIZ

The United Emirates of Orb/Clyne Faction
GAT-X103 Buster Gundam, GAT-X105 Strike Gundam, MAW-01 Mistral, MBF-02 Strike Rouge, MBF-M1 M1 Astray, ZGMF-X09A Justice Gundam, ZGMF-X10A Freedom Gundam

Main Vehicles

United Earth Sphere Alliance
Battleship Archangel class, TS-MA2mod.00 Mobius Zero, TS-MA2 Mobius, MAW-01 Mistral, FX-550 Skygrasper, Battleship Aegis class

ZAFT
Agile, Bosugolof class, Connected Armored Vehicle, Eternal , Gool, Infestus, Land Battleship, Laurasia class, Lesseps , METEOR, Nazca class, VoLPHAU

The United Emirates of Orb/Clyne Faction
Heli, Aegis class, Archangel class, Eternal, Izumo class (Kusanagi), METEOR

What are the differences between the Coordinators and the Naturals? 36

Coordinators are a breed of genetically modified humans. Naturals are normal human beings. Coordinators are endowed with superior mental and physical abilities, and their numbers have increased since human beings have increasingly migrated into space.

Coordinators tend to live mainly on colonies known as PLANT, and make their first appearance in the series as members of the ZAFT forces. ZAFT pilots Athrun, Yzak, Dearka and Nikal are all Coordinators, as is Alliance pilot Kira.

Naturals live on Earth and are divided by race, religion and social systems. In the story, most are on the side of the Alliance.

There are also Naturals with artificially enhanced abilities. These are products of experiments using artificial micro-implants in the brain and glands conducted by Alliance forces with the aim of producing specialized pilots. Those enhanced in this way end up with pow-

See Glossary
PLANT

ers of endurance and reaction speeds increased to the maximum,

These Naturals are also exposed to a form of brain-washing that allows them to discard all fear of battle. Through these modifications, they emerge as extremely ferocious opponents. And, as a result, they have superior piloting skills to Coordinators.

However, they also come with a weakness. If they do not take their regular Gamma dose, these super Naturals experience severe withdrawal symptoms. This was originally a built-in safety switch by which they could be controlled by their creators. Three such enhanced Naturals that make appearances are Olga, Kroft and Shani.

See questions

7 38 39 50

What is the Bloody Valentine incident that manages to ignite the war in space?

37

The Bloody Valentine incident is an Alliance nuclear missile attack against PLANT Junius 7 that takes place on February 14, hence the name.

Junius is destroyed in the attack, which comes soon after the Alliance's declaration of war. 243,721 pepole are reportedly killed in the attack, including Lenora Zara, the mother of Athrun.

The Alliance has also been in an ongoing dispute with the PLANT authorities over their demands to establish an independent economic zone. This now spills over into a full-fledged armed clash in the wake of the Bloody Valentine incident.

The story begins in AC 71.

See Glossary
PLANT

See questions
36

Model: HG Aile Strike Gundam
Scale: 1/144
Built by toga

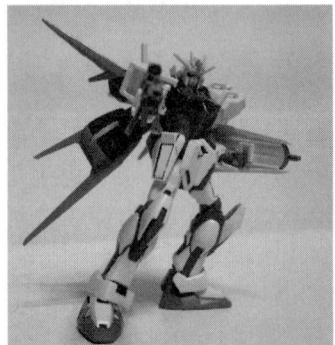

What is SEED?

38

S tanding for "Superior Evolutionary Element Destined-factor" , SEED is a hypothetical factor, the existence of which has never been proven. However, those who acquire SEED are cited as being capable of advancing to a higher level of humanity. In this sense, it is close to the concept of "newtype" that exists in the previous Gundam series.

There is no connection between whether a subject is a Coordinator and whether they develop SEED.

Indeed, as can be seen in the cases of Kira, Athrun and Caggali, SEED is more likely to be associated with the sudden appearance of superhuman fighting powers following specific causes or stimuli. This is evident for the first time in the destruction of the Eighth Fleet.

See questions

2 7 36

Gundam File   011

Gundam Goes to College

In April 2003, Japan's Kanazawa Technical University took the unprecedented step of introducing a course on "The Creation of Gundam."

Open also to junior high school and high school students, the two-year 20-lecture course aimed through discussion, research and presentations to improve the thought process of those attending. The ultimate goal, however, was to help lay the groundwork for students who would later join Japan's industrial world.

Through the theme of Mobile Suit Gundam, the classes explored the necessary environments that give rise to works of entertainment, and how these products may influence future technologies and societies.

In the first year, students studied the present world. Lectures were given by staff members of Sunrise, Sotsu Agency and Bandai on how anime ideas are conceived, and how these ideas are then realized not only as on-screen entertainment, but also as merchandise.

At the end of the first year, an event was held to which over 600 people, including members of the public, attended. Both Yoshiyuki Tomino, the creator of Gundam, and Harutoshi Fukui, the author of Turn A Gundam, took the stage to answer questions under a barage of camera flashes.

The second year introduced the future in the form of Gundam's Universal Century. In this, the technologies, such as robotics and energy sources, that shape this world were discussed and pondered over.

Without getting too academic, it's enough to say that, through lectures given mostly by key players in the animated masterpiece, the students were brought as close to the Gundam world as they could ever have imagined.

What are the ZAFT forces? 39

The acronym, ZAFT, stands for "Zodiac Alliance of Freedom Treaty", the military arm of PLANT Supreme Council.

ZAFT forces are made up of Coordinators, genetically enhanced human beings with superior capabilities that they use to develop MS, which allow them to seize the initiative in the ongoing conflict.

There are a number of interesting features unique to the ZAFT forces. All its fighters are volunteers, and most have other occupations. Despite a system based on absolute merit, and the fact that it is an army, there are no ranks within its forces.

The army is bound together by its shared Coordinator beliefs. However, each unit takes the name of its leader, such as the Zara Unit. This practice serves to establish a command network, with the whole entity coming under the command of the Council.

See Glossary

PLANT Supreme Council

See questions

36 50

Model: GAT-X303 Aegis Gundam
Scale: 1/144
Built by enocci

What is the United Earth Sphere Alliance? 40

The Alliance is known as OMNI Enforcer, an organization of countries that oppose ZAFT. Because it is comprised of numerous races and peoples, it is often derided for its lack of cohesiveness and vitality. And while ZAFT has put it superior capabilities into developing and operating mobile suits tempered to a variety of environments, OMNI has no mobile armor, and is at a great disadvantage at the outbreak of war. This is the reason for OMNI's secret development of five Gundam - to combat the enemy MS. But, immediately, four of them fall into the hands of ZAFT.

See questions
39 43 50

Model: ZGMF-X10A Freedom Gundam
& ZGMF-X09A Justice Gundam
Scale: 1/144
Built by enocci

Model: GAT-X103 Buster Gundam
Scale: 1/144
Built by enocci

What is the Neutron Jammer? 41

The Neutron Jammer is a ZAFT device developed to nullify the impact of nuclear weapons and nuclear pulse engines. (It appears to work by capping nuclear reactions.)

In SEED there is nothing comparable to the Minovsky Particles that existed in the UC period. However, because the Neutron Jammer has similar qualities, which are capable of jamming radar and radio waves, there has been a great rush to develop a battery-powered mobile suit.

The Gundams created by OMNI are designed to counter the Neutron Jammer's awesome power, and are mounted with Phase Shift (PS) armor, a cutting-edge technology.

See Glossary
UC
Minovsky Particles

See questions
3 39 42 43
50

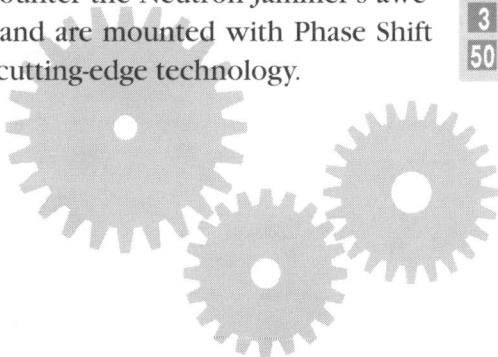

Model: GAT-X131 Calamity Gundam
Scale: 1/144
Built by enocci

What is PS armor? 42

P S stands for "Phase Shift," a new form of technology used in the armor of Gundams developed exclusively by OMNI. When the Phase Shift system is initiated, the Gundam armor transforms into a near-invincible galvanized metal. This enhanced material is capable of nullifying the impact of almost any weaponry discharged at the Gundam body.

PS armor is immensely more protective than MS plated with the standard armor. In fact, PS is only succeptible to attacks by beam weaponry or other Gundams themselves.

Rapid loss of energy is the battery-powered Gundam's greatest failing. To avoid this, the PS system can be deactivated when not required. When activated, the Gundam changes color, denoting the surge of energy.

However, extended battles can soon sap the Gundam's energy, just as exposure to beam-based weaponry can. This weakening sets off a phase shift-down.

See questions
41 43 50

Gashapon

Gashapon are an essential part of modern Japanese culture. Gashapon can be found almost anywhere, from supermarkets and candy stores to drive-ins and game centers. Gashapon come in all colors, Gashapon appeal to all ages, Gashapon are unisexual, areligious, borderless. Gashapon are Gashapon.

Insert a 100-yen coin in the machine, turn the knob, and out drops a plastic capsule the size of an egg with a little toy enclosed. This is Gashapon!

Named after the "gacha-gacha" noise that is made when the handle is turned, Gashapon became popular some 20 to 30 years ago, when kids discovered they could commandeer toy stores with little more than a 20-yen coin. In those halcyon days, the big prize was an eraser in the shape of a super car. Oh, how innocent we were...

Nowadays, of course, prices have risen and erasers have been superceded by highly detailed anime figures. Of these, Gundam's human characters, albeit with grotesquely swollen heads, are proving the most sought-after. Known as "Machikore Gundam 2", the series of 10, which includes such notables as Amuro Ray and Giren Zabi, has been snapped up as much by adults as kiddies.

With Gashapon, the pot-luck element leads to much gnashing of teeth, as one 100-yen coin after another can deliver the same character over and over again. Enter the Internet. Websites now offer, at considerably more than 100 yen, the opportunity for avid collectors to complete their Machikore 2 set by purchasing one (or all) of the 10 characters. Anime stores are also muscling in on the Gashapon market, with complete sets for sale. Are Gundam's Gashapon days numbered?

How does OMNI differ from the United Earth Sphere Alliance? 43

The United Earth Sphere Alliance (UESA) is the overall term for all nations on Earth, while OMNI is an Earth-based international organization created in place of the United Nations and refers to the military arm of the organization. Its official name is Oppose Militancy and Neutralize Invasion Enforcer (OMNI Enforcer). .

The most influential of the countries on Earth is the Federal Union of the Atlantic, which covers much of North America and extends deep into the south. Other states include the Eurasian Federal Republica and the Republic of East Asia. Not all nations on Earth are members, nor are the relations between the member countries always smooth.

As a result, OMNI is a mishmash of forces gathered from each of the nations represented, with many resultant internal disputes.

In addition, there are also some neutral states, such as the United Emirates of Orb, and even pro-PLANT/anti-OMNI governments.

See Glossary
PLANT
United Emirates of Orb

See questions
40

Model: GAT-X252 Forbidden Gundam
Scale: 1/144
Built by enocci

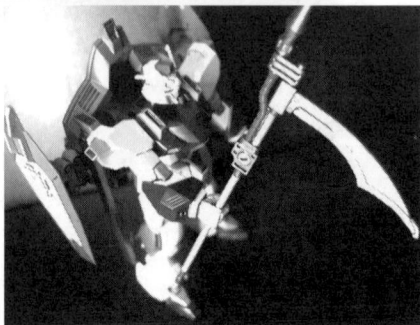

Who is Kira Yamato? 44

Kira Yamamoto is Gundam SEED's lead character and an old friend of Athrun. He is a student on Heliopolis, but becomes pilot of Strike Gundam following ZAFT's surprise attack. He later volunteers for the military and is made second lieutenant.

Kira is a first-generation Coordinator, but lives on Heliopolis to escape the dangers of war.

Following his spontaneous initiation into the world of piloting, he becomes a worthy fighter aboard the Archangel battleship.

His superior fighting skills lead him to notch up an array of battlefield exploits during the many confrontations, all while still a civilian.

Even as a Coordinator, he seems to possess extraordinary abilities, such as rewriting operating systems during the heat of battle and resetting ground environment to sandy terrain. He pilots both the Strike Gundam and the stolen ZAFT Freedom Gundam.

See Glossary

Heliopolis
Strike Gundam
Archangel
Freedom Gundam

See questions

36 39 50

Model: UMF-4A Mobile GOOhN
Scale: 1/144
Built by enocci

Who was the first Coordinator, George Glenn? 45

George Glenn had many titles: star football player; MIT graduate at the age of 17; Olympic silver medalist; ace airforce pilot; aerospace engineer; legendary hero who left an indelible mark on the world of Gundam SEED.

However, Glenn's story really begins on a mission to Jupiter, for it was then that he discovered his DNA had been altered; that he was different to other people.

He coins a new term to describe himself - "Coordinator" - linking the present and the future, and publicly reveals the detailed process for DNA modification so that others may follow in his footsteps.

This is the origin of the Coordinators, those genetically enhanced humans that have different qualities to naturally created people, or "Naturals."

Seven years later, he returns to Earth, bringing with him Evidence One. He quickly moves to establish the Coordinator research

See Glossary

Evidence One

See questions

36

institute PLANT, where he spends much of his time on experiments.

However, an anti-Coordinator movement takes hold, and Glenn is eventually murdered by a young assassin.

See Glossary
PLANT

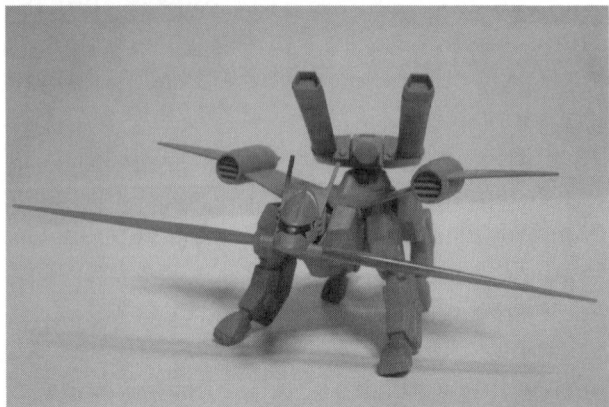

Model: TMF/A-802 Bucue
Scale: 1/144
Built by toga

What is the true identity of the masked Raww Le Klueze? 46

Raww Le Klueze is leader of the Le Klueze Unit. As commander of Athrun and his cohorts, he leads the operation to seize the Gundams and later pursues Archangel. As a leader he is endowed with superior powers of perception and judgment, and is a skilful pilot. However, his character is cold, calculating and cunning.

Nobody has ever seen his face, as he always wears his mask when meeting people. There is also a deep and long-standing rivalry between him and Mwu La Fllaga, enabling each to sense the other when close.

Raww is in fact a clone, created by the father of Mwu to continue his work. With this in mind, his one desire is to put an end to "the earth, with its never-ending greed", and he encourages the rift between Naturals and Coordinators through a chain of hatred, hoping one day to sit in judgment over all human beings.

See Glossary
Archangel

See questions
36

Gambling on Gundam

As the recession in Japan continues to bite, gambling is booming. This is especially so in the pachinko parlors up and down the country, where pinball and slot machines of every style soak up millions of dollars each day.

Anime and manga have long been popular themes for pachinko machine makers, and Gundam has certainly not been overlooked. For players with balls of steel, there's the pachinko machine "CR SD Gundam." For reel enthusiasts, there's the slot machine version "SS Gundam."

One man, lost in his own world of cigarette smoke and metallic noise, had this to say: "I was a big Gundam fan as a kid, so playing this particular machine makes me remember all those good times. The machine looks cool, but what I like most is the sounds it makes, which are straight out of the Gundam series."

Gundam slot machine

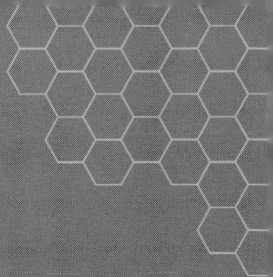

And more...

Mobile Suit Gundam F91 (1991, Shochiku)
Director: Yoshiyuki Tomino
Production: Sunrise
115 min
Flyer (7×10 inch) $1.00

Gundam the Movie (1998, Shochiku)
Director: Yasunao Aoki, Mitsuko Kase,
Takeyuki Kanda, Umanosuke Iida
Production: Nippon Sunrise
140 min
Flyer (7×10 inch) $1.00

What other Gundam stories are there apart from those in this book?

This book covers four Gundam titles - Mobile Suit Gundam, Mobile Fighter G Gundam, Mobile Suit Gundam Wing and Mobile Suit Gundam SEED.

However, there are many other titles based on the Gundam concept. These can be broadly split into two groups - main works, which include those directed by the original creator of the series, Yoshiyuki Tomino, and secondary works.

Main Works

*Mobile Suit Gundam (TV & theater versions)
Mobile Suit Gundam 8th MS Team
Mobile Suit Gundam 8th MS Team Millers Report
Mobile Suit Gundam 0080 War in the Pocket
Mobile Suit Gundam 0083 Stardust Memory
Mobile Suit Gundam 0083 The Last Blitz of Zeon

*Mobile Suit Zeta Gundam
*Mobile Suit Gundam ZZ
*Mobile Suit Gundam Char's Counterattack
*Mobile Suit Gundam F91
*Mobile Suit Victory Gundam

Secondary Works

Mobile Fighter G Gundam
Mobile Suit Gundam Wing
Mobile Suit Gundam Wing Endless Waltz
Mobile Suit Gundam Wing Endless Waltz -
Special Edition
After War Gundam X
Turn A Gundam
Mobile Suit Gundam SEED

See questions
51

*Directed by Yoshiyuki Tomino

Mobile Suit Zeta Gundam describes the world seven years after the One Year War, and the battle between the anti-federation AEUG and the Titans.

Following the war, an elite police force known as the Titans is established within the Earth Federation forces. However, because of the Titans' oppressive regime, AEUG is formed to oppose it.

The story opens with AEUG seizing the MK-11 prototype mobile suits from the Titans. In the confusion, the hero, Kamille Bidan, sides with AEUG.

A full-scale attack on the Federation HQ, Jaburo, ensues, and Amuro Ray also joins with AEUG. The war turns into a quagmire with the participation of the remnants of Zeon, the axis forces.

Mobile Suit Gundam ZZ begins in the immediate aftermath of Mobile Suit Z Gundam with a war between the anti-federation AEUG

See Glossary
One Year War
Mobile Suit

and Neo Zeon.

The final episode of Mobile Suit Z Gundam saw the battleship Ahgama, which had lost many pilots and been badly damaged, dock at the space colony Shangri-la for fuelling and repairs.

Judau Ashta, the story's main character, lives on Shangri-la, where he runs a junkyard. Together with his friends, he plans to steal Z Gundam from the Ahgama, but gets caught up in the war when a Neo Zeon battleship turns up.

Captain Bright of the Ahgama invites Judau to join his crew. Judua is cool to the idea at first, but eventually joins after learning that

Model: Dioramas"Volcanic Planet"
Scale: SD
Built by RUN

his younger sister has been taken by Neo Zeon forces. The fight shifts to Earth, then back to space.

Mobile Suit Gundam Char's Counterattack takes place some five years after Mobile Suit Gundam ZZ, and tells of the final face-off between Amuro Ray and Char.

After defeating Neo Zeon, AEUG fuses with the Federation forces. However, AEUG is by this time corrupt, and there has been little change in the state of the Federation. Char breaks with the Earth Federation to become leader of Neo Zeon, and embarks on a war against Federation forces.

The clash between Amuro and Char is reminiscent of their most famous duel during the One Year War, and it ends with a shocking climax.

It is interesting to note that the mechanical design for this series was the responsibilty of Hideaki Anno of Studio GAiNAX, who later went on to produce Evangelion.

Mobile Suit Gundam F91, while being a continuation of the previous series, is very much a new story, as the period in question is many years ahead, and there are few overlapping characters. It was produced by the same team that created the original Gundam

In the world 30 years on from Char's rebellion, the prolonged period of peace has weakened the Earth Federation. A new force, Crossbone Vanguard, attacks the Federation-built colony Frontier Side. The Federation forces struggle to battle the hardened Crossbone Vanguard, and civilian casualties mount.

Seabook Arno, who lives on space colony Frontier IV, manages to escape with friends in mobile suits, but ends up piloting a battleship as there are not enough surviving pilots.

Mobile Suit Victory Gundam follows the expansion of the Zanscare Empire on space colony Side 2, which is rapidly becoming a religious state under the empress Maria Pia Ammonia. The empress sets out to invade Earth in order to spread her beliefs.

But the Earth Federation is too weak and conflicted to effectively respond, and it is the resistance movement League Militaire that rises to the fight.

Usso, the lead character, lives on Earth, and joins the battle at Woowig near where Katejina lives. He sides with the League Militaire out of concern for her safety, and although he fears the Zanscare guillotine, he vows to overcome his foe.

See Glossary

Space Colony
Side

The battle is carried into space, where one Federation unit cooperates with the League Militaire.

We discover, however, that it is Fonse Kagatie who controls Zanscare from behind the scenes, using Empress Maria as a puppet. We are introduced to the Motorad fleet, and the ultimate weapon of the entire Gundam series - Angel Halo. This battle fortress is powered by tens of thousands of civilian psychickers and controlled by the supernatural powers of Empress Maria. With this, the Zanscare Empire plans to carry out a bloodless psychic genocide by attacking the very minds of Earth's inhabitants.

The story moves to a climactic ending.

See questions
1 2 5 9

Model: Dioramas"Fight Back"
Scale: SD
Built by RUN

Why is there an episode where Sayla has no lines?

49

I n Dakar's Day, episode 37 of Mobile Suit Zeta Gundam, Sayla Mass makes a cameo appearance, watching Quattro's speech on a pocket TV. But despite the fact that they are both former crew members of White Base, she doesn't utter a single word. This has long been a mystery for many Gundam fans. However, the reason is very simple. The episode was recorded when Haruka Inoue, the voice actor narrating the part of Sayla, was on holiday in India.

See Glossary

White Base

See questions

5

Model: FF-X7 Core Booster
Scale: 1/144
Built by Komochi-Shisyamo

155

Gundam File 014

SD Gundam: Size Doesn't Matter

The Japanese viewing public had to wait for Superior Defender GUN-DAM FORCE to cross back over the Pacific. First launched on Cartoon Network on September 1, 2003, the motley crew of squashed mobile suits only reached Japanese TV in January, 2004.

As is immediately obvious from their rather diminutive statues, the members of GUNDAM FORCE are quite different from the Gundam we've all come to love and respect. At only 4.5 to 6.5 feet high, mobile suits just don't get any cuter. But looks can decieve, as they certainly kick ass when given the chance.

SD Gundam first came onto the scene in 1987 as "Bakusho Senshi SD Gundam" in the pages of the manga Comics Bon Bon. They were the creation of animator Hajime Sato, whose concept was "to have fun with the Gundam world." The comic series proved popular with elementary school boys and soon made its way onto celluloid in the form of OVA and films. Finally, it's been reinvented for the small screen.

The story depicts the future city of Neotopia, where robots and humans coexist. That is until the Dark Axis arrives from another dimension with the aim of conquering Neotopia. The city moves to defend its habitants, both human and robot, and creates the Gundam Force.

Sunrise, the producers of the original Gundam saga, made its 3D computer graphics debut with Superior Defender GUNDAM FORCE, throwing over 60 different mobile suits into the mix that, together with the amazing graphics, makes this a show not to miss.

Does the concept of mobile suits change from series to series?

Gundam is not a robot, but a "mobile suit." In the robot animation that existed in Japan prior to Gundam, the hero was invariably an individual robot that was sent out week after week to battle villainous organizations in one-on-one conflicts.

However, if you stop and think about it for a moment, it seems illogical to have a single robot. If the robot was designed and made by human beings, it follows that more can be produced in the same way.

It was the emergence of the mobile suits that changed the one-robot anime plot. Simply put, it is possible to mass-produce MS in the same way as we mass-produce tanks and warplanes. As long as you have the design and the facilities in which to produce them, you can make as many MS as you like.

Superficially, MS look the same as robots. However, they are based on an entirely different concept. And it was probably a manifestation of pride in this concept that had the creators of

See Glossary

Mobile Suit

157

the series name them "mobile suits" and not simply "robots."

However, with the launch of Mobile Fighter G Gundam, the concept of mass-producing mobile suits began to be less important, and there was a switch to having individual MS appear throughout the series in much the same way as super robots once did.

Model: Turn A Gundam
Scale: SD
Built by RUN

The story of Mobile Fighter G Gundam in particular is based on the concept of mobile suits fighting as representatives of their nations, hence the Gundam Fight proxy war. This required the construction of single, superior mobile suits.

Shows that followed also used the G Gundam idea of introducing several individual Gundams throughout the series. So much so in fact, that it became less and less important to even refer to them as mobile suits. Fans of the original Gundam are probably gnashing their teeth in frustration at the latest series, where there is little difference between mobile suits and robots.

See questions

11

Gundam File 015

GunPura

The first plastic Gundam models, known affectionately as "GunPura," hit Tokyo toy stores in August of 1980. Even though Mobile Suit Gundam had faded from TV screens some six months earlier, the models were an immediate hit. So, when the first feature-length Gundam movie was released, the GunPura boom exploded, with fans lining up outside toy stores from the break of dawn to get their hands on the latest models.

The craze only got hotter following the release of "Mobile Suit Gundam III: Encounters in Space." In 1983, the first of the mecha model series "Mobile Suit Variation" (MSV) came out, feeding a hunger unprecedented in the plastic model market. Soon, a whole new niche had been carved out. No longer were buyers simply fans of Gundam - now, it was GunPura collectors that were driving sales skyward.

Unsurprisingly, each new Gundam series gave birth to a new GunPura series. In 1990, the first of the "High Grade Model" series was produced, with state-of - the-art technology used to refine the 1:144 scale models. Since then, newer technologies have led to waves of re-releases and upgrades.

In 1995, to celebrate 15 years of GunPura, the ultimate in scale models was created under the banner "Master Grade Model." With this, fans that had long ago grown out of modeling returned in droves, igniting a second GunPura boom that continues to this day.

Completed models that appear in this book can be viewed at the following Web sites:

JikoManzoku GunPura
http://www.h2.dion.ne.jp/~go-two/
By Komochi-Shisyamo

Moeru Kobo GunPura Seisakusyo
http://www.geocities.co.jp/Playtown/4002/
By toga

Model Runner
http://www5d.biglobe.ne.jp/~RUN/
By RUN

Seedkko Club
http://enocci.hp.infoseek.co.jp/
By enocci

Machine Head
http://homepage1.nifty.com/akm/
By AKM

Who is the creator of Gundam, Yoshiyuki Tomino?

51

Born in Odawara in 1941, Tomino cut his teeth at Mushi Productions, the anime studio established by Osamu Tezuka. He became technical director, and is remembered from that period for putting out the most continuation cards ever for the Astro Boy series.

After a scandal forced him to resign from Mushi, he found work as a director at the TV commercial production company his girlfriend worked at. Before he had time to make his mark, however, the head of the company died, and so he bounced back into anime work.

Forced to ply his trade as a freelance technical director, he worked on jobs that required him to "just bang out as many continuation cards as possible, regardless of whether they were any good." He quickly became known as "Senbongiri" ("Quick-hand Tomino") for the speed by which he worked.

Although famous for the Gundam series, Tomino was involved in a number of early projects, such as Osamu Tezuka's TV production of

Triton of the Sea in 1972.

Little progress had been made on Triton, and it was Tomino and other Mushi members that created the original story.

The final scene, which sees a reversal of good and evil, has attained legendary status in the world of anime. Tezuka even added a proviso to the anime that states he himself did not create the televised version of Triton.

Some years later, Tomino participated in the founding of Nihon Sunrise (now known as Sunrise), a company created by the staff of Mushi Productions following its bankruptcy.

He director the first original Sunrise project, Muteki Chojin Zanbot 3, which resulted in a merchandising smash hit.

Muteki expanded the storyline of Triton of the Sea while adding its own rougher edges. It proved to be a runaway hit with anime fans.

Mobile Suit Gundam was launched a few years later, and with its eventual unprecedented success, he became the man of the moment.

Building on the Gundam boom, the very next year Tomino directed The Ideon, which has become legendary for its philosophic and religious themes.

Tomino was now set to ride the wave of the second anime boom and continue to produce hit after hit.

In 1982, after changing his name from Yoshiyuki to Yuki, he directed Xabungle, in 1983 Dunbine, and in the following year L. Gaim. All of these were hits, doing nothing to detract from his reputation.

Model: HG XXXG-01D2 Gundam Deathscythe Hell
Scale: 1/100
Built by AKM

However, by crossing the line into forbidden territory with the follow-up Gundam series Mobile Suit Zeta Gundam, Tomino met with mixed fan reactions, and gradually began to lose steam.

Although he went on to produce such classics as Char's Counterattack in 1988, there was no hiding the fact that his earlier brilliance had dimmed, and following Mobile Suit Victory Gundam in 1993, he decided to call it a day.

However, the 1995 to 1997 success of Neon Genesis Evangelion triggered a third anime boom. As a result, there is renewed fascination with Gundam, and Tomino's work is experiencing something of a renaissance.

See questions
47 48

Who is the Gundam designer, Kunio Ogawara?

52

Born in 1947, Ogawara joined Tatsunoko Productions in 1972 and was placed in charge of mechanical design for such anime as Battle of the Planets.

Back in those days, there was still no concept of mechanical design as an independent and separate task. Ogawara was instrumental in establishing it as such.

Even while dealing with imaginary concepts, Ogawara succeeded in molding mechanical design into a design category as real as product or industrial design.

One of the features of Ogawara's anime work is that he is known for dealing in designs that work in real life.

As well as the mechanical creations that appear in such animated series as Mobile Suit Gundam, Ogawara also designed the mechanics for the Time Bokan series.

His major works include Yattaman (1977), Mobile Suit Gundam (1979), Fang of the Sun Dougram (1981), and Soukou Kihei Bottoms.

See questions 10

Model: MG Gundam Var.Ka
Scale: 1/100
Built by toga

Glossary and Keyword Index

Glossary

Mobile Suit Gundam

A Baoa Qu

A Principality space fortress that becomes the final battleground of the One Year War.

Aggai

Official model number MSM-04, a Principality of Zeon mass-produced amphibious MS equipped with a 105 mm vulcan rocket launcher. Because of its high stealth features, the Aggai tends to be used for special missions, in particular reconnaissance. Also known as Acguy.

Beam Rifle

MS armament for mid-distance sniper activities. Fires by taking in energy from the main engine of the MS or via an energy pack. The mega particles produced via the fusion of Minovsky Particles embedded in the body of the rifle are put into accelerated oscillation by a multi-polar super electronic coil.

Big Zam

Prototype anti-ship/anti-fortress mobile armor developed by the Zeon forces. On top of its overwhelming firepower in the form of giant mega particle cannon and 105 mm vulcans, it also has I-field barrier generators. However, it is only mass-produced in the final stages of the war, and has little influence on the conflict's outcome.

Bigro

Mass-produced mobile armor for space battles developed by the Zeon forces. Official model number MA-05. Major armaments include large-scale mega particle cannons, missile launchers, a giant pair of claw-laden arms for close combat with MS. Also has explosive acceleration capabilities. Is mass-produced in relatively small numbers.

Braw Bro

Prototype mobile armor developed by the Zeon forces for newtypes. Official model number MAN-03. Capable of attacking over all ranges via the deployment of four wired psychocommu-driven mega particle gun units. It is the first set of armor to be mounted with the psychocommu system, and the first set of mobile armor developed exclusively for newtypes.

Core Booster

A Federation forces long-distance support fighter. The Core Booster is a Core Fighter with augmented distance and fire-power capabilities. Feasible for assaults utilizing mega particle cannons and multiple warheads.

Core Fighter

An 8.6 m long, 6.8 m wide, 3.2 m high, 8.9t Federation mini-fighter plane developed as an escape system for MS. High performance converted fighter model with four 25 mm machine guns mounted in the nose, and two small missile launchers mounted on the fuselage.

Dom

A MS used by Zeon forces in land engagements. Overall height 18.6 m. Major armaments include a scattering beam gun, giant bazooka and heat saber. The inclusion of hover jet thrusters in the leg section allows for high-speed motion on land.

GM

A multi-purpose mass-produced MS used by Federation forces. Official model number RGM-79. Overall height 18.0 m. Major armaments include 60 mm vulcan gun, beam spray gun and beam saber. GM is the equivalent of the mass-produced Gundams, but lacks a Core Block System.

Gogg

An amphibious mass-produced MS used by Zeon forces. Official model number MSM-03, it is the first true amphibious MS. Mounted with such armaments as a two-repeater fixed mega particle cannon and torpedo launcher. High-speed passage through water but on land maneuverability is inferior.

Gouf

An amphibious mass-produced MS used by Zeon forces. Official model number MS-07B. Major armaments include heat rod, heat sword and five-barrel machinegun. Created for use in hand-to-hand fighting. Exhibits superior speed and power to Zaku and Zaku II models.

Great Degwin

Degwin Sodo Zabi's battleship. In the final stages of the One Year War, Zabi boards the battleship and heads off to conduct peace negotiations with the Federation. However, the ship is shot down by Solar Ray, part of a plot hatched by Gihren Zabi, his eldest son.

Guncannon

A prototype MS used by Federation forces in artillery exchanges. Official model number RX-77-1. Overall Height 15.0 m. Weight 80t. Employs Core Block system. Major armaments include shoulder-mounted cannons, beam rifle and vulcan guns. Used for long-distance support.

Gyan

A multi-purpose prototype MS used

by Zeon forces. Official model number YMS-15. Major armaments include beam saber, shield, missile launcher and space mine. The external appearance of the suit resembles the knights of old. Exhibits superior hand-to-hand fighting skills.

Halo
A mini spherical robot created by Amuro Ray. Is able to engage in simple conversation and seems to understand human brain waves. Appears in subsequent Gundam series, developing into a kind of mascot.

House of Zabi
The family that becomes de facto rulers of Side 3 after the death of Zeon Zum Daikun.
23-25, 35-36

I-field
A force field produced via the application of Minovsky physics, and exhibiting the convergence effect of mega particles used in mega particle cannons. Also capable of performing a beam barrier function when output is at great volume and with no specific directional orientation, giving it powers to deflect mega particle cannons.

Magellan
Main space battleship of the Earth Federation forces. Equipped with seven twin-mounted mega particle cannons, 14 twin-mounted machine-gun nests, and various missiles. Not a single unit in the sense of White Base, it is more accurate to use the term Magellan Class. Employs capsules deployed in the base of the ship when conducting such operations as entering the earth's atmosphere.

Mega Particle Cannon
A powerful beam weapon employing mega particles produced as a result of fusion of Minovsky Particles charged with plus and minus charges. Capable of exhibiting adequate fire-power merely by focusing the weapon in a specific direction when firing, and with no need for a large-scale accelerator.

Minovsky Craft
A form of navigation system used in large-scale carriers employing I-fields.

Minovsky Particles
Particles discovered in the process of monitoring the phenomenon of extreme electrical interference when conducting nuclear experiments in space or nuclear fusion reactors. Plays a role in promoting the practical application of MS, and is capable of nullifying homing missile attacks by interfering with radio communications. A set of unique

physical properties also allows it to serve as the impetus for the development of the beam rifle, Minovsky Craft and I-field.

31-32, 42, 133

Mobile Armor

A space weapon developed with the concept of maneuverable cannon at a time when it is not possible for MS to operate beam weapons. After MS are mounted with beam weapons, it is redeveloped into a warplane with firepower that allows it to duel. Its large size makes it the ideal guinea pig for tests of such technologies as I-field.

Mobile Suit (MS)

Humanoid robot with an approximate height of 18 m. Said to originate from mini worker robots, to which a manipulator was applied. Powered by a Minovsky-Ionesco type thermo-nuclear reactor and normally equipped with an array of weaponry. The term is used to differentiate it from Normal Suits worn in space by human beings.

23-25, 27-28, 31-32, 42, 149-153, 157-159

One Week War (The)

The war fought between January 1, UC 79 and January 10. Following a declaration of war against the Federation, Zeon forces launch a nuclear attack on Side 1, 2, and 4,

killing many civilians. The colony of Side 2 falls to Earth, resulting in many deaths.

23-25

One Year War (The)

The war waged by the Principality of Zeon against the Earth Federation. The truce, after non-combatants have suffered enormous casualties, is viewed as an admission of defeat for the Principality.

23-25, 149-153

Principality (or Duchy) of Zeon (The)

The military state established by Degwin Sodo Zabi after the death of Zeon Zum Daikun. The state ceased to be a republic, assumed the status of Principality and was rapidly militarized. Since Zabi assumes the rank of Duke, some English translations refer to it as The Duchy of Zeon.

23-25, 35-36

Red Comet (The)

The nom de guerre of Char Aznable's MS. The distinctive red-color machine has a customized engine and booster.

38

Republic of Zeon (The)

The state Zeon Zum Daikun establishes on Side 3.

23-25

Side

An administrative unit composed of space clusters. There are seven on Lagrange point. Numbered Side 1, Side 2, etc.
43, 149-153

Side 3

The Side on the dark side of the moon and furthest away from Earth. Establishes independence, first as the Republic of Zeon and later as the Principality (or Duchy) of Zeon.
23-25

Space Colony

Circular residential quarters housing up to 35 million people constructed at Lagrange point. Two versions exist: "closed types" and "open types." In the former, sunlight is refracted through translucent optical pipes into a central radiant core to illuminate the inner area. In the open types, light passes through sun panels and is guided by mirrors.
33-34, 149-153

Universal Century

The newly proclaimed period that begins with the commencement of space migration. Often shortened to UC
79-80, 107, 133

White Base

Pegasus-class assault ship, constructed as part of the V Operation in the One Year War. Known as Trojan Horse by the Zeon forces, it is the first Federation ship to carry MS into battle. Serves as the mother ship for Gundam, the Guncannon and Guntank.
155

Zaku

A Zeon forces multi-purpose mass-produced MS. Official model number MS-05. Overall height 17.5 m. Principal armament 105 mm machine gun. The first MS, originally developed for work. Also known as Old Zaku.
38

Zeon Zum Daikun

The widely respected founder of the Republic of Zeon, which was established after the revolution that took place mostly on Side 3. However, he dies of a heart attack without fulfilling his major goals. His death is rumored to have been the result of a plot by the House of Zabi, but the allegations are never proved. Zeon Zum Daikun is also father of Char Aznable (Caspar Zum Daikun) and Sayla Mass (Atesia Zum Daikun).
23-25, 35-36

Zeong

A prototype MS for Federation Alliance newtypes. The last MS built during the One Year War. With the Federation forces' prestige at stake, the suit is thrown into the fray only 80 percent complete (its legs are still being developed). The main body is mounted with a mega particle cannon, and the fingers of both hands are five-repeater mega particle cannons that can be operated by a wired psychocommu system. Specially designed body with a cockpit in the head that can operate independently in case of major damage to the body.

Zock

An amphibious mass-produced MS used by Zeon forces. Mounted with such armaments as a photonmaser cannon and mega particle guns.

Zock is equipped with legs, but as they are fixed, is required to move in hovercraft fashion on land. Only three are ever produced.

Zugok/Z'Gok

An amphibious mass-produced MS used by the Zeon forces. Official model number MSM-07. Overall height 18.4 m. Its open claws reveal mega particle cannons. Also mounted with six repeater missile launchers in the head section. Uses a single cyclops style eye that can cover a 360 degree range, leaving no blind spots. Developed for high maneuverability both in water and on land.

Mobile Fighter G Gundam

Earth Chaos War

The first major war to erupt after humans migrate into space. It is with the desire never to repeat such mass slaughter that the Gundam Fight proxy wars are initiated.

FC

Future Century - the period in which mass migration to space is undertaken.
63-64

God Gundam

A high-performance descendant of Shining Gundam. With Domon as

pilot, it qualifies for the final round of the 13th Gundam Fight.
75

Gundam Fighter

A Mobile Fighter pilot representing the colonies.
67, 73, 77

Kowloon Gundam

The Gundam Master Asia pilots to win the 12th Gundam Fight.

Master Gundam

The Mobile Fighter controlled by Master Asia.

Meikyou Shisui
Translates as "Clear and Serene".
77

Mobile Fighter
Machines that participate in the Gundam Fight. MS that serve as the manifestation of the technological prowess of each of the colonies.
67, 73

Rising Gundam
The MS taken to earth by Major Urube in order to battle Devil Gundam. A brother machine of Shining Gundam and God Gundam.

Shining Gundam
Mobile Fighter piloted by Domon. It's special weapons, Shining Fingers, are capable of destroying the head section of an enemy fighter.
73, 75, 77

Shuffle Alliance (The)
An organization operating on the fringe of history that controls all fights and aims to prevent mankind from ultimate destruction. Said to have been in existence for 4000 years.
67

Survival Eleven
The eleven-month period after the commencement of the initial stage of the Gundam Fight. During this period, Gundam Fighters wander acoss Earth seeking out rival fighters to battle. Only those fighters that emerge victorious from this stage earn the right to participate in the finals.
75

Ultimate Gundam
Developed by Dr. Kasshu and his eldest son Kyoji. Originally developed with the idea of revitalizing the earth, the machine runs amok after its program is corrupted during entry to Earth's atmosphere.
63-64, 71-72

Undefeated of the East
Nom de Guerre of the first King of Hearts, Master Asia. Under the tutalege of Master Asia, Domon undergoes a decade-long training in the Master's fighting techniques.

Mobile Suit Gundam Wing

Altron Gundam

The MS retrieved by Tsubarov as Shenlong Gundam, and along with Deathscythe repaired and enhanced by the five engineers. Equipped with telescopic dragon fangs, the machine suitably bears the name of the twin-headed dragon - Altron. Substantial upgrading of weaponry is conducted, such as the beam trident being refined into twin beam tridents, and twin-mounted beam cannons fitted to the back of the Gundam.

Aries

An air and land MS used by both the Alliance and OZ.
89-90, 91-92

Artemis Revolution

"Revolution from the Moon," the successful operation instigated by White Fang results in the seizure of Tsubarov, Libra, the Lunar base and many Mobile Dolls.
113-114

Barton Foundation

A foundation enjoying power and influence on the L-3 colony cluster. Curries favor with such powers as the Alliance, OZ and White Fang, and is able to rechannel funds earmarked for reconstruction by the ESUN to itself.

Buster Rifle

Wing Gundam's key weapon.

Cancer

The new and basic amphibious OZ MS. The lack of legs allows it to maintain superior underwater speed.

Corsica Base

A major Alliance base on the shores of the Mediterranean that includes the Leo production plant. The base becomes a target for the Gundams and is almost totally destroyed. The base commander is Bonaparte, who appears in Episode 3.

Crash Shield

Another Mercurius weapon, along with the beam gun. The shield and the beam saber were incorporated into one.

Earth Sphere United Nation

The unified state established at the end of the great war with the agreement of all nations. Unlike the World Nation, which includes only the countries of Earth, ESUN includes the colonies as well.
91-92

Fortress Mogadishu

An alliance base situated on a small island in the Indian Ocean, and equipped with a powerful noventa cannon. Destroyed in an attack by Alex and the 33rd Independent Army.

HLV

The Heavy-lift Launch Vehicles, or HLVs, used to deliver troops and supplies to the terrestrial frontlines. Of low capability, but capable of navigating space.

Lagrange Points

Relative points of gravity balance, set up to avoid the impact of gravity forces from either the earth or the moon, when constructing the Sides. The term, in fact, refers not to a specific point, but an area of space in which the Sides sit, free of extraneous gravitational forces.
85-88

Lake Victoria Base

OZ base in Africa, which also serves as a pilot training facility.

Leo

The first MS introduced to the Alliance by OZ, and used as a major weapon by both.
89-90, 91-92

Libra

The super battleship constructed by Tsubarov on orders from the Romefeller Foundation. Endowed with infinitely superior fighting capabilities to the Peace Million, and equipped with Barge-class cannonry. Seized by White Fang in the Artemis Revolution and put into use as their flagship.
109-112, 113-114, 115-116

Lunar Base

The OZ base on the surface of the moon. Equipped with a large-scale manufacturing facility, at which Mercurius, Vayeate and the Mobile Doll Virgos are developed and produced. Gundam Deathscythe and Shenlong Gundam are revamped at this plant. The base is seized by White Fang during the Artemis Revolution, together with a large number of Mobile Dolls and important parts.
113-114, 115-116

Maganac

The MS used by the Maganac Corps. Developed independently by nations in the Middle East with the same arid region specifications as Gundam Sandrock. Many variations of the Maganac exist, as its specifications allow the respective pilots to customize their suit's basics. In terms of performance, Maganac is close to Leo.

Maganac Corps

A Middle Eastern military group composed of 40 well-trained mobile suit pilots and dedicated to opposing OZ and fighting for their people's freedom. Entrusted with Quattre's safety.

Mercurius

A partner MS of the Vayeate, it is designed for defense, unlike its counterpart, which is designed for attack. While using the ten planetary defense shields mounted on its back to fend off attacks, the Mercurius can also mount attacks via the installation of a crash shield, incorporating a shield and beam saber, and its beam cannon.

Neo Titanium

An entirely new material created by the weapons development division of the Romefeller Foundation in the second half of AC 195. Developed to compete with the Gundanium alloy, it boasts twice the strength of normal titanium at only half the weight. However, cost issues prevent it going into production.

Olifant

A medium- to long-term support MS used by the Maganac Corps. The body is based on the Maganac design. It is able to participate in gun battles given its powerful large-scale beam cannon. The design is basically a mobile cannon that uses hovercraft motion rather than legs. Interestingly, it has no arms.

Operation Daybreak

The coup d'etat undertaken by OZ against the Alliance. The operation entails the coordinated uprising of OZ troops, known as Specials, that are deployed throughout the colonies. Preceeding the operation, the Alliance has fallen into a state of confusion after losing its leaders, and can offer little resistance. The coup sees OZ take over the reins of world control in the form of the fallen Alliance's Romefeller Foundation. 91-92

Operation Nova

The operation in which the mass-produced Mobile Doll Virgos are dropped to earth to set in motion the Romefeller Foundation's seizure of the planet. The targets are chosen by their ability to offer substantial opposition. The Mobile Dolls are also used to destroy the Treize clique and invade the Sanc Kingdom. 89-90, 109-112

Perfect Peace People

A political body promoting universal pacificism. However, its ulterior motive is to become the sole bearer of arms, and through this rule and control human beings. Led by Victor Gaintz.

Preventer

The intelligence arm of ESUN. Operates behind a veil of secrecy to achieve its mission of preventing any and all disputes that look set to arise. All agents, from intelligence chief Lady Une down, work under code names.
115-116

Resources Satellite M02

Resources satellite used as a base by the World Nation forces during the battle between Earth and space. Mining operations have ceased by December AC 195, and the satellite has been abandoned in its orbit. The satellite is used as an HQ and a supply base during the battle. A year after the end of hostilities a commemoration ceremony is held there at which the President gives a speech.
115-116

Sanc Kingdom

A Nordic state promoting total peace, but destroyed by the Alliance in AC 182. Reconstructed in AC 195 only to be destroyed again, this time by OZ.
89-90, 109-112

Shenlong Gundam

The MS developed by Master O. After Wing Gundam, it is the most versatile MS in existence. Indeed, the inclusion of beam tridents and dragon fangs provide the Shenlong Gundam with superior hand-to-hand fighting capabilities to Wing Gundam. It also has a characteristic telescopic right arm. Shenlong Gundam is destroyed when the battle moves to space but is retrieved by Lunar Base's Tsubarov at the behest of the Romefeller Foundation, which has an underlying interest in the Gundams. It is repaired and strenghthened by the five engineers held on Lunar Base and reactivated as the Altron Gundam.

Space Fortress Barge

The foremost space base of OZ, Barge was originally constructed by the Alliance to serve as a threatening presence to the rebellious colonists. It is equipped with a powerful beam cannon, and superior maneuverability. It becomes the last remaining outpost of the OZ forces following the success of White Fang's Artemis Revolution, but it too eventually falls to White Fang.
113-114, 115-116

Specials

A special MS unit set up by the

Romefeller Foundation, which went from supplying the Alliance with MS to supplying it with trained troops. Even the lowest ranking Special is given an aristocratic title and afforded the rank and privileges of an Alliance lieutenant.
85-88, 89-90, 91-92

Sweeper Group
Space nomads who make a living by retrieving and recycling space debris. While having no central command structure, the group maintains strong linear links.

Tallgeese
The prototype for all MS that appear in MS Gundam Wing. Sometimes called the prototype Leo, it is the first battlefield MS to be developed by the five eccentric engineers two decades prior to the development of Gundam. Equipped with adequate functions and capabilities to be able to fight and win under any conditions. However, such a burden is placed on the pilot that it is never put into practical use. The technology developed in the making of this MS is used in creating such MS as the Leo and Aries.
91-92, 93-94, 95-96, 109-112

Taurus
An MS developed by OZ for use in space. Mounted with variable capabilities and capable of accumulating battle data. Taurus is infinitely superior to Leo, and is later revamped with the Mobile Doll System.

Tragos
A mid- to long-distance support MS used by the Alliance and OZ. Appearing often throughout the series, Tragos moves via hovercraft and is equipped with cannons on both shoulders. There are also versions that are propelled by legs and some not equipped with cannon.

Treize Clique (The)
Treize Khushrenada is the OZ commander famed for protesting the Romefeller Foundation's decision to put Mobile Dolls into battle as they lack the human qualities of loyalty and honor. Because of this stance, he is placed in solitary confinement at the Foundation's HQ. This leads to a split between Foundation and Treize supporters, initiating a series of skirmishes between the Treize clique and the Foundation.
89-90, 91-92, 113-114

United Earth Sphere Alliance
Set up in AC 133 with the intention of resolving the disputes which continue to plague UESN. Alliance forces use their overpowering military superiority to contain such dis-

putes. However, that military might itself becomes one of the major causes of Operation Meteor in AC 195. UESA is destroyed by the OZ-inspired rebellion in AC 195.

85-88, 89-90, 97, 99, 101, 113-114, 115-116

Wing Gundam

The variable MS developed by Doctor J and constructed by anti-OZ elements on colony L-1. Features a buster rifle with powerful destructive powers and is highly maneuverable when transformed into Bird mode. The most versatile of the MS sent to Earth. A built-in beam saber in the shield, a vulcan gun and a machinecannon makes it a capable close-up fighter.

101, 109-112, 115-116

Wing Gundam Zero

The first Gundam of the AC period, it is developed by the five engineers who flee OZ after developing the Tallgeese. The design serves as a blueprint for all future Gundams but never gets further than the drawing board because of the extremely dangerous capabilities it encompasses. The capabilities of all five subsequent Gundams are inferior to Wing Gundam Zero. However, Wing Gundam Zero is eventually built in AC 195 by Quattre, driven by his anger at the death of his parents.

The cockpit is mounted with the Zero System, which serves to heighten the abilities of the pilot, but can also disorientate his thought patterns.

95-96

World Nation

The world state established by Relena Peacecraft, representing the Romefeller Foundation. The aim of World Nation is to promote total pacifism on Earth, where disputes continue between fellow states. World Nation is later seized by Treize.

X-18999

A new colony within the L-3 colony cluster. Completed in AC189 as an Alliance military base. The Barton Foundation is greatly involved with X-18999.

Mobile Suit Gundam SEED

Alaska Base

The major Alliance base. Under the control of the Federal Union of the Atlantic, and the command of the Joint Supreme Headquarters Alaska. Because of this, it is sometimes known as JOSH-A. Becomes the target of ZAFT's Operation Spit Break in the latter stages of the war. However, it is self-destructed by the activation of the underground Cyclops System, which destroys the ZAFT forces as well.

Archangel

An Alliance mobile suit carrier equipped with the latest in technologies and piloted by Murre Ramius
139, 143

Artemis

The military space fortress of the Earth Alliance's Eurasian Federal Replublica, situated on L-3. Equipped with the ultimate defense system, called "All-encompassing lightwave defense band", which prevents the penetration of either lasers or bullets. Known as the "Artemis Umbrella" because of its appearance. Practically invincible while the barrier is activated, the downside is that activating the barrier also prevents the fortress from mounting an attack.

Asia-Oceania Allied Nations

One of the Earth-based anti-Alliance union of states. Formed around the nations of the Australian land mass and surrounding areas. Important ZAFT ally.

Blue Cosmos

A radical organization promoting anti-Coordinator ideas. Led by Murata Azrael, Blue Cosmos is, seemingly, an anti-Coordinator political lobbying group. In reality, it incites acts of violence and bloodshed against Coordinators.

Cosmic Era

An era name used by both the Alliance and PLANT.

Cyclops System

A subterranean weapon of mass destruction used by the Alliance. The principle is the same as a microwave. Results in the destruction of 80% of the forces ZAFT throws into Operation Spit Break. The Alliance learns of the operation and, as a result, activates the system from deep within its Alaskan base.

Desert of the Dawn

A guerilla group composed of civilians and opposing ZAFT from the deserts of Libya. Friendly neither towards Alliance forces, they do, however, cooperate with the Archangel when it attempts to escape to the Red Sea after being attacked by Andy Waltfeld and his men.

Equatorial Nations (The)
One of the neutral group of nations. An economic alliance of South East Asian nations immediately below the Equator, though each individual country is responsible for its own military and foreign policy. As a neutral bloc, it is able to maintain economic relations with both the Alliance and ZAFT.

Evidence One
A fossil, apparently, of a winged whale, which proves life came from outer space. Discovered by George Glenn on his mission to Jupiter. Becomes the symbol of hope for the Coordinators.
141-142

Federal Union of the Atlantic (The)
A member of the Earth Alliance. A federal state covering North and South America, and member of the PLANT council. Maintains a massive military presence which forms the core of the Alliance. To compete with the MS of ZAFT, it joins with Eurasia and other members of the Alliance to develop the Archangel and five Gundams in top secret. But four of those five Gundams are seized by ZAFT.

Freedom Gundam
The ZAFT MS piloted by Kira Yamato in the latter part of Mobile Suit Gundam SEED. Incorporates new technologies, such as Phase Shift armor, and is powered by a nuclear engine. Equipped with a Neutron Jammer Canceler, which allows the suit to use a nuclear fission reactor and function almost indefinitely. The Gundam is mounted with a beam cannon on its back, along with a rail cannon on each hip.
139

Genesis
The definitive ZAFT weapon, which fires a massive Gamma ray laser cannon that directly shoots out the energy of a nuclear bomb. Has the power to wipe out all living creatures that happen to be within its vast range. Is thought capable of destroying the surface of the planet if fired at Earth.

Gungnir
ElectroMagnetic Pulse weapon used by ZAFT. Using pressurized electronic elements that can be produced only in space, these weapons are then destroyed at a quick rate by igniters set up close by to produce a huge electromagnetic pulse.

However, the EMP has no effect on the human body, destroying only electronic components.

Heliopolis
The raw materials satellite of the neutralist Orb situated on L5. Made up of a combination of cylinder-type colonies - seen frequently in past Gundam episodes - and a resources asteroid.
139

Morgenroete Corporation
An armaments corporation with close ties to Orb. Developed the Archangel and five Gundams in top-secret at Heliopolis on the orders of the Federal Union of the Atlantic. A number of Coordinators are on the Morgenroete staff, apparently making high-tech contributions to the firm.

Onogoro Island
An island belonging to Orb, and situated north-east of Papua New Guinea. Shared by Orb forces and the Morgenroete Corporation, the island is under such tight security that it cannot be monitored even by satellite. Serviced by a mass-driver launch pad.

Operation Spit Break
An operation late in the war, proposed by Patrick Zara, that involves descending to Earth. It is originally considered as part of Operation Uruboros as an invasion of space port Panama, but the target is switched to the Alliance HQ in Alaska the very moment the operation starts. This change in target doesn't receive the authorization of the Council, an omission not communiated to the troops taking part in the operation. Zara is secretly in touch with the clone Klueze, and orders him to carry out the operation, but Klueze leaks information of the operation to the Federal Union of the Atlantic.

Operation Uruboros
A ZAFT operation at the outset of war to invade the earth. The operation is aimed at bottling up the Alliance forces on Earth, and succeeds in seizing Alliance ports near the Equator, such as Panama, Victoria and Kaoshung.

Organization of South African Unity (The)
One of the non-Alliance groups. A pro-PLANT/anti-Alliance economic and military union in the southern half of Africa, though for all intents and purposes under the control of ZAFT.

PLANT
Short for Productive Location Ally of Nexus Technology. The Coordinator space housing complexes.

Positioned as new-generation complexes, to differentiate them from earlier colonies. Constructed by Coordinators, with about 100 units at L5. The word PLANT implies new-generation colony, while also carrying the nuance of a gathering of Coordinators. Originally under the control of the earth, PLANT becomes an independent state at the outset of the war.
123-124, 125, 137, 141-142

PLANT Supreme Council

The supreme decision making body conducting the administration of PLANT. Comprising 12 members elected from 12 cities.

129

Strike Gundam

A Mobile Suit developed in top secret by the Alliance, and the only suit not to fall into ZAFT hands. Eventually piloted by Kira Yamato.
139

United Emirates of Orb

A neutral country on Earth that exists under the policy of "No invasion of other states, no invasion of Orb by other states, no interference in disputes between other states". Maintains a powerful military force to enforce that policy.
137

KEYWORD INDEX

From character goods to on-screen anime stars, the MYSTERIES AND SECRETS REVEALED! series brings you everything you never knew and more about your favorite anime and manga characters. Compiled in Tokyo, Japan, home of otaku culture, this series is unofficial and unrelenting in its quest to unearth the mysteries and secrets behind some of the world's most popular anime!

Coming soon in the MYSTERIES AND SECRETS REVEALED! series

The Dragon Ball Z Legend
The Quest Continues

Akira Toriyama's Dragon Ball series is loved by fans all over the world. However, so many mysteries remain unsolved... What happened to this or that character? Who and what are behind the Dragon Ball creations? Where and when do the stories take place? From the history of the Tenkaichi Tournaments to the Secrets of Nameck, this book explores the world of Goku and the people and creatures that inhabit his world.

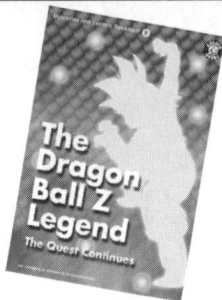

$11.95 ISBN 0-9723124-9-8 May 2004

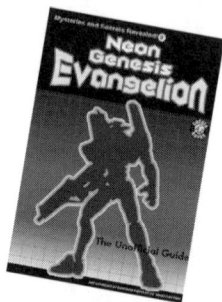

Neon Genesis Evangelion
The Unofficial Guide

Neon Genesis Evangelion was one of the major anime works of the last decade. Director Hideaki Anno used the medium as no one had before: as a means for personal expression and for exorcising private demons. However, the TV show and subsequesnt feature films left many hardcore anime fans scratching their heads in wonder. This book sets out to answer the numerous questions that the complex and endlessly fascinating characters raised: from the Angels to the Evas to Shinji and his estranged father Gendo.

$11.95 ISBN 0-9745961-4-0 June 2004

The Lupin III File
Secret and Confidential

Since the '70s Lupin III has been a star of the anime screen. This amorous French master thief travels the world in search of easy riches and big rip-offs. The Lupin III File uncovers the secret life of this crafty cartoon hero. Who is he really? Why does he live the life he does? And what about the other characters that fill this action-comedy world? Everything you ever wanted to know about anime's most-loved crook can be found within the pages of this book.

$11.95 ISBN 0-9745961-7-5 July 2004

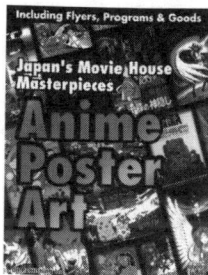

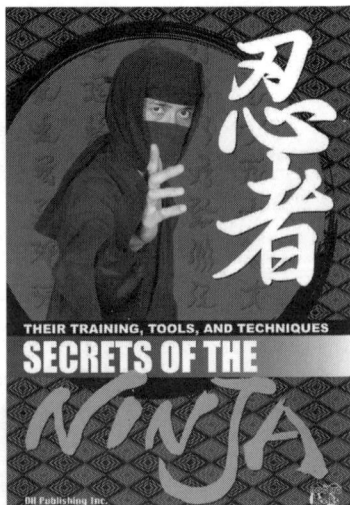